Bet On Yourself

FROM ZERO TO MILLIONS

Dr. Vernard L. Hodges

TROJAN FARMS REAL ESTATE LLC
BONAIRE, GEORGIA

The Publisher
Trojan Farms Real Estate LLC
102 Starlight Drive
Bonaire, Georgia, 31005 USA

Bet On Yourself: From zero to millions
Dr. Vernard L. Hodges—1st ed.
ISBN-13: 978-0692985960 (Trojan Farms Real Estate LLC)
ISBN-10: 0692985964

Contents

For my son, Vernard Hodges II

Those who lead, read

—Anonymous

INTRODUCTION

Why?

I learned early that school wasn't set up for people like me to succeed. I wrote this book to give hope, knowledge, and encouragement to people with limited options. You have to scratch and claw to educate yourself. Refuse to be a victim of your surroundings. Get up every time life knocks you down. Refuse to take no for an answer. Never quit, despite how hard life gets. If you're going to do well in life, bet on yourself, because if you don't, then who will?

When I was growing up in a rural Georgia trailer park our family had very little. Our options were limited. My friends and I all dreamed of becoming superstar athletes or famous rappers. But most of us ultimately went into the military, labored at the local bus factory, went to jail, or got killed. My story is different.

This book is my story of how I bet on myself, and the lessons I learned. How I overcame huge obstacles to live the life. I was a smart kid, but not "school smart." There are other kinds of smart; street smart, hustle smart, survival smart. And then there are the smarts my friends and I used growing up in the rural south to overcome a common perception that we weren't good enough. I was a failing student in high school. Yet I went from picking peaches for $0.70 an hour in the hot Georgia sun, to gaining admittance to one of the most prestigious professional schools in the country, and then on to become an owner of multiple veterinary practices. I became a community leader and philanthropist. I taught myself to become a successful real estate entrepreneur. I started with one single family home investment and turned it into a multi-million dollar real estate portfolio producing rents of over six figures monthly. In this book I show you how I did it, the method I used, and one you can use, too.

All young people struggle to know what to do with their lives. What's next? What am I gonna be? How do I get there? How do you know? What don't you know? If you're searching for the answers, I'll show you how I did it, and how you can live the life you deserve.

When I was young, I hung out with crack dealers in the bad part of town. I saw what "easy money" did to my community. It was easy come, easy go. That lifestyle never pans out for long. Nothing trumps hard work. Those who took the easy road had the nice clothes and cool cars. They were popular with girls. It looked like they had it all figured out. To a teenage boy, it was a glamorous lifestyle, but it didn't take long before I could see that lifestyle was a road to nowhere.

In a small town like mine, we thought our community was the world. When we were young we only saw what was in front of us. Yet I've learned the world is a much bigger place. I didn't know it at the time, but opportunities to live a better life exist— if we have guidance or know how to find them. I always looked for—and found—mentors. I had different mentors at different stages of life. I remain grateful to them for their support, protection, and encouragement.

I am so thankful because it would have been easy for me to become a statistic. And that's where I was headed. But I was fortunate because people saw things in me I did not yet see in myself. Too many black men from my background are behind bars. African-American male role models were scarce when I was growing up, and they still are. Because so many kids, like my son, look up to me as a role model, I feel the need to share my life experiences. That's the reason for this book.

School never taught me the essential things in life; how to get along with different kinds of people, how to be your own boss, how to expand your options, how to find a mentor and the big one— how to manage money. I devote Chapter 11 to *Money 101*. As a kid, I had no idea what a bank does, what the stock market is, how to write a check or the vital difference between good debt and bad debt. These are the essentials of life.

I've always loved animals, always wanted to do something that involved working with them. I never thought I could become a veterinarian. But I did. If you'd asked me 20 years ago whether I would write a book, I would have just laughed. Yet here it is.

Part I of this book is my struggle to find my path in life. My fraternity brothers of Omega Psi Phi taught me life-long values of manhood, scholarship, perseverance, and uplift. My summer internships took me from a catfish farm in Mississippi to the foothills of the Himalayan Mountains on the other side of the planet in Nepal. I tell the story of how I got into vet school and how my partner, Dr. Terrance Ferguson, and I got fired from our first job and then started our own successful veterinary practices. I learned the value of paying attention to my surroundings and to shut up and listen. If there is one message in this book it is the value of teaching yourself by getting into the reading habit.

Part II of *Bet On Yourself* starts with my first adventures in real estate. I learned to teach myself about real estate investing, and the important concept of cash flow. As you'll see, that didn't stop me from making mistakes. But I hit more home runs than pop flies. With perseverance, I've become the equivalent of a 300 hitter, and most 300 batters are Hall of Famers.

I made millions in the stock market, only to lose it, make it back again, and then some. I'll teach you how I did it, and hopefully, you won't make the mistakes I did.

In 2004, my son was born, Vernard Hodges II. The joy of his birth coincided with my severe losses in the stock market. It was a low point for me. But looking in that crib at the exact replica of me made me realize there was no way I was giving up. Becoming a father made me realize the importance of doing the right thing when no one is looking. I tell how I bounced back from near ruin, and share some of what I learned about investing for a better life. There are valuable lessons here about business, connections, real estate wealth creation, and the pleasure of helping others. It's surprising what you can achieve if you try. I hope you find this book entertaining, useful, and ultimately uplifting. That's why I wrote it.

Dr. Vernard Hodges

October 2017
Warner Robins, Georgia

PART I

CHAPTER 1

Motivated by shame

I failed the ninth grade. For a poor black kid like me, the system is set up for failure. Yet today, I'm a successful entrepreneur and a respected veterinarian with a thriving practice. This is my story of how I went from zero to millions.

I grew up in Fort Valley in Central Georgia. It's a poor community. At the time we didn't know how poor we were. I never met my father. And I haven't to this day. I wouldn't know him if he walked into the room.

I was raised by my mother and stepfather. Dad was of Japanese extraction and grew up in Hawaii. He was from a middle-class family, far different from the one I was used to. I'm forever in his debt for the way he took an interest in me. He taught me a lot of things. He pressured me to do better, taught me to be a man of my word, to love animals, and to lend a hand whenever it was needed. But he didn't teach me to be a good student. I was at best a C- student. My mom came from a very poor family. She gave me love and support. She encouraged me to work hard and get a job.

We lived in a trailer park. Our single-wide trailer had a two-foot by a two-foot hole in the kitchen floor. Dad fixed it by covering it with a sheet of plywood. I hated that hole. It was so embarrassing. I tried many tricks to camouflage that piece of plywood so my friends wouldn't see it. I often wondered why my dad never tried to put a laminate floor covering over that hole. I guess it just wasn't important to him. He would rather spend his money making sure I had life's necessities.

I remember being about eight when I asked him, "Dad, why don't I look like you?" I was a dark-skinned little chubby kid with short hair. He had lighter skin, and dark black wavy hair, like the guys I saw in karate movies.

"Look at me," he said "I'm a descendant of samurai warriors. You're my special samurai warrior, God made you perfect." My dad was my hero, he gave me confidence. There was nothing I felt he couldn't do. We didn't talk about life much. He always led by example. He gave me a middle-class perspective on life. He showed me a different way of thinking from the culture most of my friends and I were living in. He was always interested in animals, and that's how I became interested in them.

Dad was a great philosopher, but a poor businessman. He wasn't financially successful. But I don't think he really ever wanted to be. Every time he had a talent or product that might lead to success, he always gave it away for free. He was a jack-of-all-trades and would try just about anything. He wasn't built to be put in a box as somebody's employee. He was his own man.

Dad spent his life's savings on a down payment to purchase 40 acres of land. His dream was a cattle farm, and this investment would make it happen. He was doing well with the project. The farm was flourishing, but there was a problem. Mama cows were having babies as planned. People raise cattle to sell calves. But it would break his heart to sell the babies away from the mother. He couldn't stand to hear the mamas' sad mooing as their calves were taken away to market—so much for his cattle business.

His next venture was to raise goats. He read that goats were gonna be the next big thing. But they ate everything on the property and left a trail of destruction behind them. They even ate the bark off the trees. The goats had to go.

He tried earthworm farming. The trouble was it was very labor-intensive. Dad was inventive; he could take two pipes and make a pontoon boat. He even tried to build a harvester for earthworms. He was smarter than me. He had lots of ideas. But the difference is this: I learned to monetize my ideas.

He built a koi (ornamental fish) pond. We were probably the only place in America to have a koi farm in a trailer park. After he purchased the 40 acres, he bought a bulldozer to excavate more ponds. At one point we had more than 30 ponds and thousands of koi. He spoke at koi clubs across the Southeast. He gave lots of advice. The reason he didn't make money was he gave his knowledge away for free.

Years later, after my veterinary practices had gotten some success, I told him I would make his fish farm successful. I set up a limited liability corporation (LLC). I went online and studied how people sold fish. He knew a lot about koi because of his training when he was a kid. He learned from his father and grandfather. I was confident we would make money. Koi are expensive. They sell for between $4 and $3000. It's rumored the most anyone paid for a koi was $2.2 million.

I set up a website and marketed the fish. When orders came in I would tell my dad how many and what color fish we needed to fulfill the order. We inspected them, put them in a big plastic bag half filled with water, and then filled the rest of the bag with oxygen, sealed it, and put it in a big box for next-day delivery. I received many orders from all around the world, but we had difficulty filling them. Dad was holding up production.

Dad would always want to find the perfect fish. I told him you can't ship the ten best fish in the world every time. Ten good fish will do. He was meticulous. Perfectionism was a problem. Because he wanted to wait until he found the perfect fish from our ponds, we would lose orders, customers, and (my) money. Fish food for 30 ponds ain't cheap. It wasn't about the money for him. He would give them away.

In the end, I said, "We won't worry about trying to sell koi. For you, it's not a business. It's your hobby. That's okay, I'll fund it. You just play with your ponds, fish, and bulldozer."

***

When I failed ninth grade, I didn't tell my parents. I was fourteen that summer of 1985. I had a job picking peaches. It was a hot, exhausting job. I was paid $0.35 a bucket. I made $0.70 an hour. It's a job Hispanic migrant workers perform now, but back then it was how we poor black kids made our money for school clothes.

The peach fields were near the school. I'd go off to work on my bicycle in the mornings, but instead of going to the field, I enrolled in summer school. Nobody knew. Later, my mom asked, "How come you're going to work every day, but you don't have any money?" Then I had no choice but to tell her how I screwed up at school. I was embarrassed. I didn't want to repeat that grade. I figured out a way to make it right on my own. I think she saw I wasn't as dumb as I looked, and I had some pride, so she let me finish.

The Trap

About the time I matriculated high school, rap music was coming on MTV. I loved it. And I still do. All of us would rap on the bus on the way to school. Back then, the kids, at least some of my friends, were having some nice things, shoes, and clothes like the rappers in the music videos.

My friend (I'll call him Marvin) was one of my best boys. He was a big guy, well-dressed, a gifted athlete, and always looked well-groomed. Marvin had wads of money.

He probably made six times what the teachers did. I knew his money wasn't from picking peaches. So I asked him where he got it. He said, "Crack." I didn't know what crack was. This wasn't New York City. This was 1980s rural Georgia.

"Listen, man," he said, "What you do is take $10. Buy some crack, and sell it to somebody else for $20. We call that doubling up." It was a lot faster way to make money than working in the peach field. Marvin is in prison now. He's still my friend and to this day, I send him money to make sure he's good. But I'm glad I didn't follow that easy money path he did.

I grew up with Marvin. I watched his money and power grow. I was his sidekick. I watched him get into multiple confrontations over his turf. He always came out on top. Back then guns weren't as prevalent as they are today. But people would beat each other up. I was fortunate I didn't have to sell crack. Marvin's group took me under their wing. Because Marvin vouched for me I got to go to the Trap.

I had street credibility hanging with Marvin and his crew. The Urban Dictionary defines a trap as a place to buy and sell drugs. It was a cool place to be for us teenagers. This is no longer a drug area today because most guys went to jail, or were killed. The Trap was in what we called the "Bottom." It was at the bottom of an incline of 25 feet near the train tracks. There was one way in, and one way out. Police cars couldn't get across the tracks.

Kids worked as lookouts in the top entry. When they hollered, "5-0!" that meant the police were coming. We ran. We'd cut through vines and escape over the train tracks.

A trap is usually in a bad part of town. Everything was on sale there; cars, TVs, guns, jewelry and even houses. People were desperate for money to buy drugs. It was a dangerous place. People got their stuff taken often. Some were beaten up. But it was where all the pretty girls were. It was where the cool cars were. It was where all the action was. I saw people make a lot of money.

One problem we African-American males have is big egos. There's immense pressure to be the biggest and the baddest. That's just part of our culture we grow up in. When I was growing up neighborhood basketball was the big thing. The better athlete you were, the cooler dude you were thought to be, and that made you popular.

When we were playing basketball in the Hood, the best guys got to play. When you're next-up, if you suck, and your team loses, you don't play again that day. How different is that from today where everyone gets a participation trophy. But this isn't how it is in real life. Everyone doesn't get a trophy for showing up. There were valuable lessons to learn from being in the Trap. I learned respect. On the basketball court, or on the football field, play well and you earn respect. That's just like life.

I'd hang out in the Trap and be cool. I watched the wild happenings. I wanted those cars with their custom hydraulics and fancy paint jobs. I especially wanted those pretty girls to hang out with me. But the reality was different. I'd catch the school bus to the Trap, and later have to find my way home. No pretty girls wanted to hang out with me.

In those days, people still received welfare checks. The first of the month, some people would spend their whole welfare check in the Trap, in about two hours. Thursday nights was when the Trap saw the most action. It would be jumping like Jordan. Business was booming. Blue Bird Corporation, a bus manufacturer, paid its employees on Thursdays. Some would cash their checks and head straight to the Trap. Tens of thousands of dollars were made by kids barely old enough to drive.

Two worlds

The Beastie Boys, Run-DMC, Eazy-E, and The Fat Boys were just starting. We all wanted to be rappers. None of us ever were. I'd still love to be a rapper.

Success in my community was working at Blue Bird. A lot of my friends worked there. Some of them still do. When I was growing up, the work at Blue Bird was hot and demanding. There was no air conditioning. It's hard physical labor, welding, putting on tires. But if you got a job there, you were considered to be doing great since it paid almost twice as much as most jobs in my hometown.

But there were hurtful things there too. Through the grapevine, we found out there was a swimming pool at Blue Bird. We never even saw it because it was for whites only. After long grueling days of football practice in the Georgia sun, we would all go home and cool off with our water sprinklers. Our white teammates would go chill at the free private Blue Bird pool. It was just another humiliation we learned to accept growing up in the Deep South.

My high school prom was also segregated. That was the way it was even into the 1990s. There was a white prom. And there was a black prom. I have no idea where the whites had their prom. We went to classes together but any co-mingling at the prom wasn't tolerated. We raised money for our black prom. Those were just the times. It made me feel inferior, but as a group it made us love each other more and become stronger. It's been over 20 years and my class still meets regularly for functions and trips. We've created a life-long bond; a togetherness that can't be broken.

Until recently my mother lived in the home I grew up in. A year ago, I went to the local hardware store downtown to get supplies to fix a plumbing leak at her house. I've been in that store many times as a kid. But it had been a while since I had visited the store. I forgot what it felt like to be followed around as if I would steal something. It brought back those old childhood memories of being inferior. But then I smiled, said a small prayer to God, thanking Him for how far he has brought me. And then I thought to myself: *If I wanted to, I could buy this whole damn store.*

You can overcome those feelings of inferiority, or let them destroy you. What doesn't kill you makes you stronger. I decided a long time ago, I could be angry, I could be bitter, or I could educate myself, work hard, and bet on myself.

Most people in the Trap went to jail, into the military, or got themselves killed. I was very fortunate that it didn't end badly for me. Or that my mama didn't kill me. If you knew my mama, and the foolishness I did, I'm lucky she didn't. One time I was holding some bags of crack as a favor to Marvin. I hid them in my mama's washing machine. Later she threw the clothes into the machine and turned it on. That was the end of Marvin's crack.

"Where's my baggies?" said Marvin.

I was embarrassed and scared. "Well, I hid them in the washing machine, but my mom did a wash." He was angry at first, but not for long. There was so much money being made. Easy come easy go. He eventually lost most of his money to lawyers.

When I was in college, Marvin would give me money to help with college expenses. He would say, "Man, you're gonna make it. You're gonna do something big one day. I don't want to see you out in these streets. Just go to school, work hard, and make good grades. If you need help, I got you."

Marvin always came through when I needed help, as I have for him. I still remember him knocking on my college apartment door one night. He said, "I need you to hold this paper sack." I counted $290,000 in that bag. That was a lot of money in 1993. He knew he could trust me with it. But when he got caught he lost it all.

I still tease him he should have just given it all to me. Anyone could make money in the Trap in those days. A kid could get out of school, catch the bus, go to the Trap, and make $500 to $600 in an evening. That easy money destroyed a whole generation.

People rode around booming loud music in their high-performance cars with the flip-flop paint. It was the cool thing to do. But the police seized those cars in drug raids. It was a heavy price to pay, loss of money and freedom. The cars were turned into DARE (Drug Abuse Resistance Education) cars enforcing the message that drug dealers will forfeit their glamorous lifestyle eventually, and crime doesn't pay. I was very tempted to sell drugs as a teenager, but it never panned out. I saw this was a lifestyle with no future.

Limited options

For most of us, the options were Blue Bird, the military, or, rarely, college. Yet there were exceptions. My friend Tim Watson was a straight-A student and a gifted athlete who won a scholarship to college. He had a career in the NFL and then opened his own business. He was a positive influence. Tim came from a solid family. We would talk about school and academics and how we could make it out of the Hood.

Marvin was always an expensive dresser. He'd have the latest designer clothes, bling, and Nikes.

My other friend, Marcellus, wore a plaid shirt and Levis every day. All three of us were athletes. We played football together. Marvin and Marcellus were good athletes, both with college offers. I was average.

Marcellus's mother died at a young age. He was raised by his sisters and they would try to keep us both in line. His father was mean to him. Most people around town knew his father was an alcoholic. Yet Marcellus made good grades, didn't sell drugs, or hang out in the Trap. He hated me hanging out there with Marvin.

Marcellus was offered a scholarship to go play football, but he was hell-bent on going in the military and taking his best buddy—me—with him. He would pick me up in his big hulking Buick LeSabre. It was a gas guzzler. We would only put about $5 in it at a time. We ran out of gas in that thing so many times. We called it the Deuce and a Quarter. That car got us a ton of places though. We hung out at the local teen center, bought our first alcohol together, went to cookouts, and generally hung out and had fun. But Marcellus did a good job of steering clear of trouble.

Army

Marcellus lived with his uncle. Uncle Lee was doing well, retired from the military, and was Marcellus's biggest influence. He was a nice guy and got us thinking about a possible good life in the military.

Marcellus and I met army recruiters at a high school campus booth. In their dress uniforms, they made a positive impression. We learned that they would train us to be ready to tackle the world.

I was 16 years old. It was a spring day when a busload of us kids arrived in Atlanta. We were there for the day. First, they gave us a good meal. Then they gave us a short history of the American military. They took us into a huge amphitheater and showed us movies of how great our futures could be. They told us how we could make America proud. It made us all feel patriotic. For a country boy who had seen little, this was cool.

Marcellus and I scored well on the Armed Services Vocational Aptitude Battery (ASVAB) test in high school. Our recruiter indicated that we had qualified to do the job we wanted: Medics. But when the Military Occupational Specialty (MOS) paperwork arrived, it was bait and switch.

Our recruiter promised us the world, and how we would benefit from the GI Bill. We'd have medical benefits for life. We'd make good money, and maybe even become generals. His job was to get us to the Military Entrance Processing Station (MEPS). Staff at the MEPS were friendly. But the MEPS were looking to fill any open jobs the army needed. Nowhere on that paperwork said anything about medics.

The job they initially offered us was to get on the back of a truck and make smoke. Or, we could be infantrymen. They told us these were the only jobs available now. We could sign now and switch later after basic training. Making smoke didn't appeal to us. One thing the Trap taught me was, *don't fall for the ol' banana in the tailpipe trick.* If Marcellus hadn't been there for support, I think I would've signed. There's definitely a value of connection to someone you trust and respect. Because there were two of us, we held out for the job we wanted. We didn't sign.

It was back on the bus for us.

Several months later, our recruiter came to my house. He was sharply dressed as ever. He told my mother I was smart and I would be a great asset to the military. If I still wanted to be a medic, he said he had worked it out, and there were open slots for us to become medics. So, this convinced me to give MEPS another shot.

The second time we went to the Atlanta MEPS, we experienced the same procedure; bus ride, sitting down to a good meal and watching movies about opportunities in the military. Only this time we were ushered into a small room. On the desk was paperwork saying we would become medics. We signed, and then it was time to get back on the bus.

Some weeks later we returned to the MEPS center for our first swearing-in. It was an emotional experience. I felt patriotic. I felt like I was about to become the guy I was trying to be all my life. It felt good. It was a relief to know what I would do with my future.

Receiving our duty stations made it all feel real. We were scheduled to report to Fort Jackson in South Carolina in July 1989.

But I never went into the military.

CHAPTER 2

A new path

My godmother, Miss Rosie Petties, was in charge of developmental studies at Fort Valley State University. She had nothing against me going into the military. But she wanted me to give college a try. She told me about the Middle Georgia Consortium, a workforce development agency. She told me how they would pay for me to take the SAT and pay for my first semester in college.

If it hadn't been for Miss Pettis I would never have understood this resource existed. I thought: *If it won't cost me anything, I'll try it.* Miss Pettis filled out all the paperwork and made it easy for me.

The SAT wasn't that hard. Okay, I barely passed. But I got in.

People usually come to school in the fall. But we were on the quarter system, so I attended summer quarter. I could pledge a fraternity in the spring quarter because I attended summer school, fall and winter quarters. I became the youngest to pledge the Mighty Upsilon Sigma Chapter of Omega Psi Phi. It's been one of the greatest decisions of my life. The men of the Mighty U.S. are a special group of people, and I can't imagine where I would be without them.

Brotherhood

Fraternities don't advertise for members. You must be asked to join, or somehow express your interest. The thing about black fraternities is when you join it's for life. Jesse Jackson, Michael Jordan, and Shaquille O'Neal are all in my fraternity. If we happen to meet up or see each other out, it's as if we've been lifelong friends. Unlike the Rushes or public post for membership, you must know someone to get into fraternities at most Historically Black Colleges and Universities (HBCU). Joining turned out to be a major event in my life. Choosing the right group of men to be part of makes all the difference in the world. The friendships I made boosted my confidence. And some have turned into life-long associations. Here's how it happened to me.

I was in a music class. I was sitting behind an older guy who was in the fraternity, Pipe. Every day he had on his fraternity jacket. I was mesmerized by that jacket. I wanted it. One day I got up the nerve to talk to him and said, "I want to be part of your fraternity." He looked at me. He didn't smile. He said, "Get me the final." I thought to myself, *how can I do that?* And to this day I don't remember how I got that final paper. I think it was a girl who had already taken the test, or someone who worked in the professor's office. But I got the test.

So I went back to class, and said: "Hey, man, I got the test."

He still never smiled. He looked at me, and said, "This better be the damn test."

And it was the test! Half the fraternity brothers said I was too young to get in. But Pipe stood up for me because I could walk the talk. He persuaded the group to give me a shot. I made the cut. I was a new *Lampado* along with my six brothers who went through the initiation with me that spring of 1989.

A Dean of Pledges is responsible for running the pledge program of a fraternity chapter. To get into the fraternity we had to prove our worth. Over a ten-week period, we had no time to spare. The lamp is a symbol of our fraternity, so and we were Lampados. We had to run from class to class with a heavy wooden lamp around our necks. We wore camouflage pants and heavy boots. There was almost no time to take a shower, and we stank. This period was so demanding we hardly had time to eat. All seven of us lost weight, a lot of weight, between 10 and 20 pounds. We were kept so busy that we suffered from sleep deprivation.

Yet, as we hurtled around campus reciting pledges, girls would stick money in our pockets for food, since we looked scrawny and having lost so much weight from running around doing our big brothers' commands. The pledge program trains new members to become productive fraternity brothers and to follow the four cardinal principles: manhood, scholarship, perseverance, and uplift.

My dean of pledges was nicknamed Smoke. I can never thank him enough for the life lessons he taught me. He never smiled. But that was just his personality. He was a mentor. He helped me ask the right questions. He'd say, "Look, boy, are you doing any school work?" This was an important question for a young man with nothing but fun on his mind. When joining a fraternity there is a propensity not to do much school work. There were always opportunities to have fun. It's easier to party than it is to do school work. Smoke was looking out for me. And he wasn't the only one.

Most people thought my fraternity was the best on my campus. I was an only child and this was an experience to assimilate with a group of other men. Some did the right thing. And some didn't. I learned new habits, some good and some bad. And there were people to help keep me in line. I was still in my hometown and the Trap was just a few miles from my fraternity house. There was some jealousy from my hometown guys because I was now only hanging with my fraternity brothers. I had to walk a line between both.

I was a 17-year-old kid in one of the most popular fraternities on campus. I'd gone from being a semi-shy goofball to being "the man." By joining the fraternity, I became popular overnight. It gave me instant status. I went from maybe one girl wanting to date me to many wanting to know who I was, all because I put that fraternity jacket on.

We'd make fraternity road trips. I would liaise with fraternities at other small colleges around the state. That way

I met many people and made valuable connections. The beauty of it was we never had to pay for anything. We just showed up.

Eventually, I moved up in the fraternity. I was flexing my new entrepreneurial muscle by organizing events. There was only ever a first time at any one venue. We had a huge fundraising event called the Mardi Gras. We needed to rent space. After a while, we ran out of places to rent. Our parties were too wild. No one ever wanted to rent to us again. The toga parties got bigger. Thousands of people came. We made thousands of dollars.

My fraternity brothers and I got into trouble for doing something crazy on campus. Our academic advisor said, "No Mardi Gras this year." We didn't want to lose all this money and we had to do something, so I came up with the idea of calling it a "Call It What You Want to Party." We printed up the flyers and it was a great success. We rented the 6-million-square-foot Georgia National Fairgrounds and Agricultural Center in Perry. I organized charter buses to bring people to and from the event. People wondered what was going on but I was using my business mind to make it happen. I learned by doing.

I knew we were in trouble when one guy tried to bring a horse into the party. I told him that there's no way you can bring in a horse.

The following Monday my academic advisor called me into his office. Just two weeks before he had given me an award for my fraternity work. Now, he didn't look so pleased. He shook his head.

"I said no Mardi Gras."

"We didn't have a Mardi Gras."

"Well, what did you have?"

"We had a Call It What You Want to Party."

I was suspended with my fraternity brothers from participating in any fraternity activity for six months. College was a great learning experience.

HBCUs are an indispensable resource for the African-American community. They were established before 1864. Originally, there was no other option for black people to attend college. They've always allowed admission of all races, but their purpose is to serve the black population.

Smaller black colleges serve people like me. Without going to an HBCU, I wouldn't have had the opportunity to move on, and eventually get into veterinary school. At Fort Valley State, there were other black men with backgrounds like mine. They understood where I was coming from and gave me learning support. But I also got help from another direction.

Dr. Davis

When I went to college I had no idea what I would do. I started by just taking general education courses and then chose agriculture as a major. It was at this time I met one of the most influential people in my life, Dr. Melinda Davis. To this day I think of her as my guardian angel. She was a Caucasian lady from Oklahoma and received her PhD from a large university. She had come to our small HBCU to make an impact. And did she make one! Dr. Davis had the single most impact on my education. She was my college advisor. She took a genuine interest in me. She wasn't just my mentor, she was my friend. Often during my free times, I would hang out in her office. Dr. Davis was a tough teacher. She was diligent, and she pushed me to do better. Thank God for her, because she believed in me when I didn't believe in myself.

One day I stopped by her office. I told her I was interested in fish, and about my experience with koi from working with my dad. She talked about marine biology and showed me some of the coursework. She suggested fisheries biology and aquaculture would be a good major for me, so I switched. I figured it's easier to learn something I'm already curious about.

After long nights of partying I missed classes a few times. My fraternity house was on route to Dr. Davis's office. On more than one occasion, she stopped by the fraternity house, knocked on my door, came in and woke me up. "Get your ass in class!" she said. But tough love was exactly what I needed. She never gave me a grade, but she always gave me love. Her care helped me believe in myself. She was mentoring me to be a college student, and so my confidence grew and my grades improved.

Learning on the job

The summer of 1989, Dr. Davis sent me to a fisheries project at the University of Missouri at Columbia.

Limnology is the study of inland waters, and I learned to sample water for phytoplankton, tiny microscopic plants.

My first road trip was the journey to the University of Missouri. There was no GPS in those days, so my dad mapped out the route on an atlas for me. I drove up from Georgia to St. Louis. And then two hours to the south, I stopped by the Omega Psi Phi fraternity house at Lincoln University, another HBCU. My fraternity brothers made me welcome, took care of me, and showed me around.

My job at the University of Missouri was working in a research lab. I learned about the properties of water, and how to sample it for microorganisms. And then there was the fieldwork. Our group gathered samples from many lakes. We often worked in remote locations. We collected samples from the 93-mile-long Lake of the Ozarks. One time, my partner told me to sit in the truck and keep quiet because some of these people had never seen a black person before. But I didn't experience any trouble, quite the opposite.

I was 18 years old. The school provided me with a beautiful lakeside two-bedroom house all to myself. I did some of the best fishing ever. I was making $14 an hour. This was a long way from $0.70 an hour peach picking. Dr. Davis made it possible for me to attend conferences put on by the Association for the Sciences of Limnology and Oceanography (ASLO). But I didn't realize what Dr. Davis was setting me up for.

Not long afterward, I went to an ASLO conference in Virginia Beach, Virginia. The program brought in minority students to the field of limnology and oceanography. This happened during school time and the conferences lasted three to five days. It was an all-expenses-paid visit – and a lot of fun.

I learned how to present papers. I learned about new topics. I ate the greatest seafood. An 18 wheeler truck pulled in with taps on the side. It was full of beer. But the main value was networking: making contacts. This is where students would network to find their next school.

Most of the ASLO attendees were PhDs, looking for students to follow the same masters or doctoral path. But that wasn't me. I had struggled with academics, but I developed great friendships. I took this opportunity to check out some nearby HBCUs.

Some months later Dr. Davis called me into her office. It was then I found out what she was setting me up for. She told me, "We will pay you $20 an hour." I thought to myself: *Now you're talking my language!* She told me about a project in Nepal for The United States Agency for International Development (USAID). But where is Nepal? I'd never heard of it. I had no idea Nepal was on India's northern border, and over 8000 miles away on the other side of the planet.

Are you Mike Tyson?

I'd never flown before. I flew from Georgia to Los Angeles and then changed planes for the trans-pacific 15-hour flight to Seoul, South Korea. From there I flew over 2,000 miles to Thailand. I was exhausted by the time I got to

Bangkok, Thailand's capital. I saw military personnel carrying machine guns. I was so tired I went straight to the hotel and slept. The hotel was the Waldorf Astoria. Someone came in to turn down my bed and put a flower on it. I was thinking, *whoa! I've never stayed in a hotel like this before.*

When I finally arrived in Kathmandu, Nepal, people stopped me in the airport. They all had the same question: Are you Mike Tyson? Back then, Mike Tyson was one of the most popular guys in the world. The Nepalese had never met someone like me or seen a black guy except on TV. And I had never met people like them. The first thing I saw was a group of poor children pressed up against the wire fence begging for money. I thought I knew what poor was, but these people were really poor. They were living on just a few cents a day.

And then there were the cows. When we were driving down the street we had to stop often because there was a cow in the road. There were cows everywhere; cows in the street, cows in the lake, cows in the store. Our USAID project was to develop a cheap protein source for the population. I couldn't imagine why these people aren't eating all this beef?

I learned cows are sacred. Nepal has no official religion. But according to the 2011 census, 81 percent of the population was Hindu, and 9 percent Buddhist. Nepal isn't the place to open a McDonald's because Hindus don't eat beef, and many are vegetarian. But most people will eat fish, the protein source we were there to help develop.

On the six-hour drive north from Katmandu we passed by raging mountain rivers and saw water buffalo used for plowing fields. Water buffalo aren't sacred, but the Nepalese don't eat them. Their milk is too important a protein source.

Finally, we arrived at our destination, Pokhara, a city on Lake Phewa. Pokhara is right at the foot of the snow-capped Himalaya Mountains and a jumping off point for people trekking up to higher elevations. A major source of income is from the tourist industry. People come from all over the world to go trekking in the Himalayas. I regret I didn't take advantage of this spectacular scenery by going on a trek.

The Nepalese are nice people. The average height for men is 5' 4,'' and for women 4' 11." The meals were also small. I was used to eating a lot of food by their standards, so I would order two meals. There was no AC in the hotel and it was hot. We were told not to use ice or drink the water. Every day, the electricity would go out for two or three hours, but I could still buy food or a Coke at roadside stands. So I was still a happy camper.

Feed a village

We chose carp for the project because they don't eat other fish, they eat phytoplankton. Lake Phewa is a rich source of carp food. At certain times of the year, water levels rise or fall because of the heavy monsoon rains. We'd take water samples to measure how well phytoplankton will grow at different levels in the lake. Then we'd know how deep to put the cages containing carp. I'd already learned to sample water, so that's where my skills came in.

In Nepal, there is the risk of contracting hepatitis A and typhoid through contaminated water or food, so the Center for Disease Control (CDC) recommends routine vaccinations for travelers. We had to take a lot of preventive medicines. And I am glad I had some with me because I was able to help Prem.

Meeting Prem was an eye-opening experience and it taught me to be appreciative. He owned a boat and was contracted to the project. Prem was 19 and married with a little girl aged three. He was so happy to see me. He was poor, had almost nothing, but he never asked me for anything. When he was curious about my Bart Simpson T-shirt, I gave it to him. His little girl was sick and they had no medicine. But I did, so I gave him some. He gave it to his little girl and she got better.

He was appreciative, and we became good friends. He took me to the foot of the Himalayas, but at the time I was more excited to see monkeys run across the road. I should have gone trekking, but I didn't. Prem was resourceful. He provided a life for his family with his boat. He never wanted to go and eat. But he always invited me to come to his house for native Nepalese food. I think he didn't have the money to eat out. He was very proud. So I tricked him into taking money for things he did for me. I didn't have much either, but I was more than happy to share the little I had with him.

The Agency ran into a problem because of the caste system. Part of the USAID project was to teach the people how to farm fish. This is where the caste system showed itself. The traditional caste system is complex and tricky for an outsider to understand. Some of the lower caste people stayed back in deference to the higher caste. I wanted to bring them forward and make sure they understood what they should be doing, but this didn't make the higher caste people happy.

But I had a job to do, I knew I was going home, and I didn't think they would beat me up. Some probably thought I was Mike Tyson. But mostly the people were delightful. This experience was life-changing for me. Despite their poverty, they are a proud people. Some people believe that life should owe them something, but that's not the Nepalese I met. They're very thankful for what they get. I cherish that learning experience. It taught me compassion and to be grateful for what I have.

***

In-between summer internships Dr. Davis arranged for me to go to my second oceanography conference in Albuquerque, New Mexico. Meeting Native Americans was an eye-opening experience. I never realized how much of a raw deal Native Americans got. I love the turquoise jewelry. They can make anything out of turquoise. I thought of myself as a minority, but I didn't think of how it is for other minorities.

Never be a quitter

That next summer I froze my butt off. My internship was from Virginia Tech. We were measuring trout stream populations and their ecosystems in the Shenandoah Valley for the U.S. Forestry Service.

The schedule was six days on, and four days off. We worked so high in the mountains that sometimes it would take us a whole day to walk up to our work location. I'd never seen clear water before. Being a country boy in rural Georgia, I used to think there were only two types of water, dirty, or red from the Georgia red clay. We measured trout populations and made topographical maps showing the elevations of the surrounding terrain. I didn't even know what a topo map was before that. I learned a lot. We estimated trout populations. We used electric shock to stun the fish, count them, measure them, give them some medicine, and put them back.

Those mountain streams are cold. We had neoprene wetsuits, but it was still freezing being in the water all day long. We lived in tents for about a week at a time. There were six of us in the crew. The others didn't mind but I hated sleeping out in a tent. The bathroom was the woods. The job application said nothing about bears. We had put our food on the end of a rope and hung over the stream so the bears wouldn't get it. You should have seen the expression on my face when they told me we had to be aware of bears.

I like being outdoors, but I like to come home after a hard day's work and watch TV. I loved the job, and the pay was good. Yet when the work was done, I was still in the woods.

No cell phone. No TV. No McDonald's. But I didn't quit, and it taught me something about myself: never to be a quitter. But I told myself, I'm never, ever, camping out in the cold woods again.

Confidence

During the next academic year, I presented a paper about our work in Nepal at the Bay of Fundy in Nova Scotia, Canada. My topic was how to grow a protein source for the local population, and then teach them sustainable aquaculture. It was called *Utilization of the Subsurfaces of Phytoplankton at Lake Phewa in Nepal.*

For marine biologists, the Bay of Fundy is a special place. I was amazed to discover the difference between high tide and low tides was 32 miles, that's as far as Macon is from Fort Valley. I learned about how the moon's gravitational pull causes tides.

Because I was interested in aquaculture, we went to a location where they were trying to farm lobster. Lobsters are expensive because they're all wild caught. They can't be farmed for profit because they're cannibals. The strange thing about lobsters is they can grow huge. When the lobster grows, it sheds its shell. That makes them vulnerable to predators. Other lobsters will eat them.

While I was in Nova Scotia, I visited the Black Loyalist Heritage Centre which tells the story of the world's largest free African population outside of Africa. Many "Black Loyalists" escaped northward to Nova Scotia after the American Revolution and set up the largest free black settlement in the 1780s.

I learned about public speaking. I presented well enough that ASLO wanted me to come to their conference. I was the only black person, and that was cool. There were three things I liked about it: it was free, they gave me a $350 stipend, and they put me up at the Marriott right outside of Disney World. They gave me an ASLO membership, too.

I looked the part of the student the PhD professors wanted. They would love to have a smart minority in their program. They would always ask me if I was interested in being their PhD student. But I knew my grades weren't good enough. Yet I was learning and gaining confidence. I was becoming a person who reads and is always learning. People believed in me.

Overconfidence

I had a place reserved to work in a lab in Florida for my last summer internship. It was a cushy job. I planned to make a lot of money. I was sure I could get the job because I had gained so much experience during my summer internships. And I did get the job after a brief interview. But I was cocky. They asked me to supply some basic information about myself, and I put it off. Because I didn't do what I was supposed to do, I got fired before I got hired. Experience alone doesn't cut it. I met with the employer when he came back to campus. I begged him to reconsider. He listened, but I never got that job back.

Despite my vow never to go camping again I found myself living in a tent for eight weeks in the woods freezing my butt off again. I got my old government summer job back through Virginia Tech counting fish populations. I took a leadership position. This time it was in the Smoky Mountains of Tennessee.

What I liked about this job was I got two checks. Besides getting a good rate of pay, we had a per diem meal allowance. I saved a ton of money because in the remote Smoky Mountains there is nowhere to spend the per diem. We ate out of cans, and we cooked meals on a little Coleman grill.

***

If Miss Pettis hadn't suggested giving college a try, I would have taken another path. I'm grateful to her and the Middle Georgia Consortium for making college possible. I'm grateful to Dr. Davis who believed in me. She gave me a chance to succeed. I learned the value of relationships in the Trap, but also through my lasting fraternity friendships, teachers, and the people at ASLO. The visit to Nepal and meeting Native Americans in New Mexico taught me compassion for those people who have less than I do.

All these experiences helped me grow. I was growing up.

One day I was hanging out in the biology building, and Philip Mitchell, a recruiter from Tuskegee University's veterinary school, walked in and did a seminar on the prestigious Tuskegee University School of Veterinary Medicine. I listened to his spiel on how great the school was and how Tuskegee University graduated 90 percent of veterinarians of color, not just in the U.S, but in the world.

While Philip was talking about the school, I was thinking this could be what I'm looking for. I thought to myself: *Perhaps I could finagle entrance to a master's program, or maybe, if I'm lucky, I'll get into the vet school.* I applied and was invited for an interview.

I told them the story about Nepal. And they liked what they were hearing. I told them African-American males are severely underrepresented in the veterinary profession, and how valuable I would be as a member. I told them about my past experiences, and the obstacles I'd overcome. I wasn't just interviewing, I was selling myself.

I had the confidence to try to cut a deal. I told them I was already a fish biologist and was sure they didn't have one applying. I would be bringing my experience to their school.

I got in. But I had a shock coming to me.

CHAPTER 3

Vet School

I had my come to Jesus moment on my first day in veterinary school. I went to the College of Veterinary Medicine at Tuskegee University (TUCVM) in Alabama, the only veterinary medical program at an HBCU in the United States.

Dr. Goyal, a distinguished teacher, arrived in class with a grocery cart full of papers. He was pushing it up and down the aisle filled with syllabus packages. He said, "Take a syllabus." I reached in and pulled out a few papers. He said, "No, no take the whole package." That package must've weighed 10 pounds. That was the moment I realized this school would be more demanding than I thought. And I was right. But I wasn't about to be a quitter.

People want to be veterinarians because they love animals. Many of us grew up around critters and love them. But when we got to our first gross anatomy class of the first year of vet school and were given a dog to dissect, for some people it was all too much. The freshman year was designed to weed out students, and the first big test of staying power was gross anatomy.

We spent the first three hours of the day in the gross anatomy lab. We called it "the pit," a cold, concrete, windowless room in the basement. Funk and formaldehyde filled the air. I never want to have to go back and do that again. They gave us an anatomy book, and a dead dog to dissect. We worked in pairs. One of us read from the book. The other dissected every vein and muscle in our dog. It was tedious work. Not everyone made it.

My second year was a lot of work. I struggled with theory. I still had a dream of being a fish doctor. After four weeks of intense study, we took a block of tests every day for the next week. But the beauty of it was, after every block of tests we had a big party. Even though I was in veterinary school, I was still a party animal.

Physiology was extremely hard for me. There's a lot of memorization and figuring out how various body systems work. I was struggling. So, when I was called before the Academic Council, I was worried. I was just scraping by. But they said they wanted me to succeed. Not everyone learns in the same way they told me, so they assigned me a tutor from the third year class. I will be ever grateful to my tutor Dr. April Woods.

Today, Dr. Terrence Ferguson is my trusted business partner. He is an excellent animal surgeon. We were good friends at Fort Valley State. He was also a good athlete, a college quarterback. We were together at Tuskegee where they paired us as big brother/little brother. Terrence was my little brother. Even though he is a slightly older, I was a year ahead of him because he didn't get good academic counseling. He made excellent grades and had a GPA higher than mine. He just had poor advisement. To succeed it's important to find someone who can help guide you through the tough times. Without the right mentor, Terrence would have stayed on the vet tech track. It was only after meeting with Dr. Davis he got on the right path to become a veterinarian.

Terrence was "Mr. Academic," and a great problem solver. I've always admired him. He leads from the front and was class president for all four years at Tuskegee. His success shows how much people admire him and look to him for leadership. I'll be saying more about him in the next chapter.

During my third year of vet school, my teachers saw I could figure out problems, so I got extra hands-on experience. They were always pulling me out of class to go on pet calls with them. That's when things clicked. By the end of my fourth year, I was making good grades, even a few A's. I won tons of awards at our senior banquet. I received a framed Norman Rockwell painting with my name engraved on it. The faculty voted me as the most proficient class member in large animal medicine. I guess the lightbulbs had come on; later is better than never.

Stop, look, listen, and think

Vet school was a challenge. On more than one occasion, I learned to stop look and listen. One day our professor took a group of six of us students on "ambulatory call." We went to a field of dead cows. It was a humid 103°F Alabama afternoon. When we got there we saw about 50 of them. Our professor asked us, "Why did all these cows die?" We looked at each other. No one had the answer. They smelled nasty. They had already started to rot. I saw a possum come out of one of their butts. It was gross.

An autopsy is performed on humans to discover the reason for death. For animals, it's called a necropsy. So we cut up the cows to discover what was going on. It was a hot, horrible, messy, stinking job. Meanwhile, our teacher was sitting in the truck laughing at us.

After a while, he called us over. "Well, have y'all figured it out?" We offered all kinds of unlikely solutions. He said, "One thing you need to learn about veterinary medicine is to stop, look, listen, and think. Notice what's happening," he said. "Look, the dead cows are all around that tree. It's hot today. What happened yesterday?"

Yesterday there'd been a storm. He said, "Look at the top of the tree." And there was the solution. The tree had been struck by lightning, and the cows had been sheltering underneath. They'd all been electrocuted. We could've saved ourselves a lot of work.

This experience taught me a life-long lesson: stop, look, listen, and think. Through hands-on experience, I could see how theory and practice all fit together. Even though the school curriculum wasn't designed for someone like me, I realized God had put me on earth to do this work.

***

In my junior year, I took the national licensing exam to become a veterinarian. I was worried because I never got great grades. I was great with hands-on and understood how to make animals better. My professors knew this, but when it came time to take a test I always seem to come up with a C.

Dr. Braye, who was on the Alabama State Board, called me out of class to come into his office. He had tears in his eyes. I thought: *Oh no, are they're going to put me out of school?*

Dr. Braye said, "Hodges, I've never been so proud of a man in my life."

"What did I do?"

"You passed the licensing exam!"

I was so happy when I went back to class. I was asked what was going on, I said, "I passed the Board!" They looked at me as if to say, no way! But I did. I was one of six out of a class of 60 who passed the first time. I had the juice! I started believing in myself again.

Mississippi catfish

My grades improved in my senior year, and my growing confidence allowed me to see more possibilities. I looked at aquaculture opportunities. There was no bigger player in the aquaculture business than Mississippi where they raised catfish.

I contacted Mississippi State because they had a summer program. I told them I was in veterinary school but I didn't quite have the grades, but I wanted to do it. I figured I might as well give it a try. They said okay.

I contacted one of my fraternity brothers in Mississippi, Dr. Walter Roberts, an older gentleman. He had also graduated from Tuskegee. He was the only black veterinarian for miles around. His farm stretched for 400 acres where he raised fish and cows. Mississippi is such a poor state; many people don't have indoor plumbing. I was a student, and I was considered rich there. He said I could stay with him, so I went down to Mississippi State University's College of Veterinary Medicine.

I worked in the laboratory at the fishery. The black workers would bring samples of water or samples of fish to the lab. It made them proud to see the only black kid working in the laboratory. But it was more of a shock to some of the poor white workers to see me there. They said nothing but I could sense their disapproval.

Catfish farming is intensive. The more fish you can raise in the least water the more money you make. Catfish ponds are huge, 100 feet by 100 feet and only 4 feet deep. Overcrowding causes two big problems: lack of oxygen, and contagious disease.

When I visited the plant I noticed a lot of machinery that wasn't being used. I later learned that machinery was brought in to fillet fish. But the workers were worried that it would put them out of a job, so they worked hard and were more efficient, cheaper, and faster than the machinery. You must do what you must do to feed your family. It was a beautiful thing to see all these middle-aged, mostly black women working, and the machines standing idle. I admired their will.

And I could see the pleasure it gave those women to see me; a young black man, working in the laboratory. I didn't know it at the time, but I was starting to be a leader. I was showing what can be done. Only later, I realized that leaders aren't born, it's something you learn.

Dr. Roberts was a character. I remember a truck driver arriving with paperwork authorizing the driver to collect the fish for sale. Before harvesting catfish, the first thing they are supposed to do is to take out a few and check they are the correct size. If they're okay, they'd back up a truck to the pond and scoop them out. But this driver didn't do that. He went ahead and took out fish without measuring them first.

Then the truck driver told Dr. Roberts the fish were too small and was going to put them back. However, putting them back wasn't an option because many would die.

Dr. Roberts said, "You've taken them out, and now you're going to take them."

The truck driver said, "No, I'm not."

The driver didn't know that Dr. Roberts had a glass eye. Dr. Roberts went back to his truck and fetched an old rusty gun. He pointed it at the driver and said, "You're going to take the fish."

The driver was now paying attention. But he didn't look scared of this old rusty gun. Dr. Roberts was raising hell and cursing at him.

And then Dr. Roberts' glass eye fell out. He caught it in the other hand. Now he looked like a wild man with a gun in one hand and his glass eye in the other.

The driver decided that he'd take the fish.

The team at Mississippi State wanted me to apply and become a PhD student, but I was embarrassed to talk about my grades. They were looking for the 4.0 GPA and I struggled to maintain a GPA of 2.5. I filled out the paperwork anyway.

As vet school was coming to an end, it was time to think about a job. At the end of my senior year, the Tuskegee bursar explained my financial situation to me. I was shocked to learn how much I owed, $70,000. I had bad credit because of a cell phone agreement I didn't understand. Who knew how important credit was? What was I going to do? I went to see my first veterinary mentor.

My mentor

Next to the trailer park where I lived stood one of the nicer houses in Fort Valley. It was about 6000 square feet and belonged to the town's veterinarian, Dr. Corker. He became my mentor.

When I was seven or eight years old I worked in his yard. Much later, after I had done some volunteer work at his hospital, he wrote a letter of recommendation that helped me get into Tuskegee. Dr. Corker started a school for veterinarian technicians at Fort Valley State University. Even though I didn't attend that program, I knew many people who did, including Terrence.

I told Dr. Corker about my situation. I had nothing lined up. I might get a job as a veterinarian at Pet Smart. I knew a few PhDs who would go to bat for me. But I doubted they would let me into one of their programs. When I talked about all this with Dr. Corker, he said, "Why don't you come over and work for me?"

It was an offer I couldn't refuse.

CHAPTER 4

Startup

In 1997 I went to work for my mentor Dr. Corker in Warner Robins, Georgia for $38,000. I learned a lot from him, but I showed him some new things I had learned, too. I was the emergency doctor. I worked almost 24 hours. That was okay because he had given me an opportunity when no one else had. I worked there for a year, and things were going well. Revenues were increasing. The following year Dr. Terrence Ferguson joined the team. Terrence had interned under Dr. Corker for almost ten years.

Sometime later I increased my veterinary salary to $55,000. But I owed much more than that in school loans. I thought to myself: *This isn't what I signed up for.* Everyone thought I was a rich veterinarian, but that was far from the truth. I could barely pay my bills and school loans. Terrence and I needed to find a better source of income.

Dr. Corker was then in his sixties. He agreed to let us buy into the business. We didn't know exactly how we would do that with no money. Both of us had a lot of debt. But we did know our hard work had an impact on the business: revenues were increasing. Every day at lunch, Terrence asked about our buying into the business. Dr. Corker was getting a little annoyed with his continual questioning. What we wanted to know when was this buy-in going to happen.

One day we got called into his office after work. Dr. Corker sat at his desk, and we sat in two chairs opposite.

He said, "Gentlemen, I think I'm going to run this practice myself."

"Are we fired?" I asked.

He said, "Yes."

This was a complete shock. I asked why, but he didn't say. There are two things I took from this meeting. First, we needed to be our own bosses. And second, how the hell did he change the locks on that building so quickly? When we tried to leave, our keys didn't work. I must ask Dr. Corker how he did that. I still tease Terrence about how he got me fired.

My cousin Jackie cried when I lost my job. She is the next best thing to a sister. She had bought a big antebellum house in Fort Valley. She told me she wouldn't charge me one dime to stay with her. I said, "I have to give you something." But she said no. She was pivotal to my success at that vulnerable time. I didn't have to worry about a place to stay, or even putting food on the table. But once I got established, and for many years after, I showed my thanks by paying Jackie's mortgage in December. That was my Christmas present to her.

A few days after the firings Dr. Corker came by Jackie's house. He was crying. I said, "Dr. Corker, what's wrong?"

He said, "I need to talk to you. I can pay one veterinarian well, but not two."

I listened, and then I went to talk with Terrence. A lesson I learned from the Hood is, always be loyal. I told Terrence about Dr. Corker's visit and the how he could only pay one of us well.

Terrence said, "You need to go back."

"I can't go back like that," I replied.

"You need to go back," he said.

I told Dr. Corker I would return to work on condition he hired Terrence until he found something else. Dr. Corker agreed.

Terrence and I returned to work for a few months, but it was never the same. We were creating a lot of value. The reason more people were coming in was to see Terrence and me. We doubled gross revenue: the practice was worth more, much more. But Terrence was still holding Dr. Corker's feet to the fire over his buy-in promise.

As I remember it, Terrence went out on vacation, and Dr. Corker said that he would pay him, but he need not come back. When Terrence called me, I realized, that's it! We must find a place of our own.

A place of our own

It takes about 15 minutes to drive from Fort Valley to Byron. I came across a little paint shop going out of business in Byron. I met with the owner and told him we'd like to rent the space. He said it was already rented. But as I was driving away, the guy called me and said, "What was it you wanted to put in there?"

"A veterinary clinic."

"Let me think about it," he said.

The building owner called me back the next day and said, "We'll rent it to you for $800 a month." We were overjoyed, but we didn't have the money to pay someone to build it to our specifications. We built it ourselves. We pooled our resources, bought wood and nails, and made it happen. For a few weeks, Terrence was doing construction while I was finishing up with Dr. Corker.

Our deadline was May 15, because that's my fraternity anniversary. All good things seem to happen on May 15, and that's the day our clinic was born. The first name for our new business was Byron Veterinary Associates. We even signed some paperwork with that name. But after a while, we thought we were taking ourselves way too seriously. Then we came up with the name of Critter Fixer. It was perfect; a catchy name that everyone loves. It fits with our laid-back country boy attitudes.

No credit

We had a building. We had rent to pay. But we needed equipment. We had a long list of expensive items. We tried to lease veterinary startup packages which included a complete set of equipment, but each time we were denied. The problem was we were poor with no credit history. I had no house. I had school debt, a Toyota 4Runner on lease to my dad, and no job. It wasn't just lack of credit history, it was worse than that. I had bad credit. We couldn't even get cages without paying cash.

We didn't know about credit. They never taught us that in college. But I had a thirst for knowledge. It was now that I started my life-long habit of reading. One book from that time stood out to me, *Rich Dad Poor Dad: What the rich teach their kids about money that the poor and middle class do not!* by Robert Kiyosaki. I learned about good debt and bad debt. The poor use debt to buy liabilities, those things that take money out of your pocket, like cars or clothes. The rich use debt (other people's money) to buy cash producing assets, like tools, or rental housing, or a veterinary clinic.

The biggest lesson I can pass on is to read. Go to a bookstore, buy a latte for five bucks, and read. I do this regularly. I read about credit. I learned that you had to build up a credit history. You need a credit card to get a credit card. It sounds crazy, but it's true. I'll say more about credit and managing money later in the book. We tried several vendors, but no one believed in us. It was time to try something different.

We bet on ourselves. We searched in the back of veterinary magazines for people going out of business, or people retiring. Finally, we found something that looked promising. We drove Terrence's old truck with a trailer all the way to Birmingham, Alabama. It was a hot drive and that truck had no air conditioning. The guy in Birmingham sold us a bunch of equipment for $4000. We had cages, an anesthesia machine, and an x-ray machine from World War II. We told him our sad story of how no one would extend credit to us, and he even gave us some extra stuff.

While we were building our Critter Fixer clientele, I got a job at an emergency veterinarian hospital in Macon. I later got Terrence hired there. It was in the Hood. Robberies were common. We kept the door locked at night. We'd work all day at Critter Fixer and then drive up to Macon at 6:30 p.m. We'd sleep in the emergency clinic. That's how we supported ourselves. We were working 24 hours a day.

In those first six months, Terrence and I did everything ourselves. We couldn't afford to hire any help. We made a couple hundred dollars a day. It allowed us to keep the lights on. If we made $500 a day we felt like we had an awesome day.

People in Byron were talking about two young black guys with the new business in town. The all-white Rotary Club asked us to come and speak at their breakfast meeting. We were nervous, but it went well. We told the Rotary Club members we were local guys and wanted to serve the community. We explained our various stories of how we became veterinarians and how we ended up in Byron. They seemed genuinely interested. A few years before us there had been a veterinary clinic in Byron but it had closed. That meant we were the only animal clinic in town.

We needed a new place to do business because we were running out of space. There is only so much you can do in an 800 square-foot building. There was no way Terrence and I could do surgery simultaneously or practice the medicine we knew we were capable of.

Riding with Hal

A big, black tinted-window Mercedes pulled up to the office the week after we spoke to the Rotary Club. The driver got out and told us somebody inside the car wanted to talk to us.

The man inside told us to get in the car. We were going for a ride. He introduced himself as Hal Peavey. Word around town was Hal Peavey's a tough businessman. He made his fortune by owning much of Byron. He owned an apartment complex. He owned a bank. He owned the shopping plaza and the grocery store. He sold land on which the post office now stands. He was a man of few words. We didn't know this guy. But he had a reputation. People told us to beware because we were so young and naïve. They thought he would take advantage of us. He got rich by having business smarts, and we feared him.

Hal had heard about us through members of the Rotary Club and told us he wanted us to stay in Byron. Terrence and I stared at each other, both thinking the same thing: *Okay, we planned on staying.* We rode around in the car as he pointed out buildings. He'd point to one and say, "How about this one for your clinic?" He pointed out several vacant lots. Our reply was always the same, "Looks fine to us." Finally, he pointed to a lot he owned behind a medical center. It was next door to a grocery store. It looked like the perfect spot. But to us, it made no difference, because we had no money or credit.

We went to his house. Even his house intimidated us. He was an imposing figure, even in his wheelchair. I believe he had MS, and I think he was an engineer by trade. Some people said bad things about him, comparing him to the covetous and manipulative oil baron JR Ewing, from the TV series Dallas (1988-91).

But Hal Peavey was a blessing to us. He wanted us to get him some architectural drawings. When you own almost everything in a small town and the mayor is your lawyer you don't need to bring in an architect, you just need a few drawings.

He asked us if we get trade magazines where we can see drawings of buildings. He wanted them so he could keep his men working before he started a bigger and more lucrative project. We shook hands.

Not long afterward, I got a call from Hal. He told me they were breaking ground on our new project. When I told my accountant about it, he said, "Man, y'all be careful. You have to watch Hal. He's a shrewd businessman."

Months go by. The building goes up. Occasionally, we look at how it's proceeding. Hal wasn't the person to belong to clubs. But his girlfriend Pat was in the Rotary Club. And that's how Hal had heard about us. She was sweet and liked us.

One day, when the building was finished, Hal says, "Are y'all ready to buy it?" At this point, we had no contract or any paperwork, just a handshake.

We say, "Yes."

He says, "How about $450,000?"

It was probably worth that much money, so I said, "Okay."

A week goes by and nothing happens.

A week later, Pat came to the office. She said, "You realize you guys can counter offer, don't you?"

"What does that mean?"

She explained that the price is negotiable.

Another week goes by before we decide how much to offer. So we come up with a figure of $205,000, and Hal agrees.

That was easy, but we still haven't got any money! Even if it was $100,000, or even $10,000 we still haven't got it. And no bank was going to give us a loan. Then I read about seller financing.

Seller financing

When an owner finances buying real estate or a business, the owner acts like a bank. Hal agreed to extend credit to us so we could buy the building. Anyone can become a lender by issuing a promissory note. It works like this. The buyer and seller sign a promissory note, often just called a "note." This is a written promise by the buyer to pay the seller a sum of money. A note is more than an informal "I Owe You" (IOU) which is just written evidence that the debt exists. An IOU doesn't have the details of repayment.

A note is more specific. It contains how the money is to be paid back, the interest rate, and when the principal amount is due. The lender can charge an interest rate higher than a bank because the lender is taking on more risk. For the lender, a note is a valuable "debt instrument." It is a promise of future payment and something he can take to the bank as collateral (if he wants to) for a new loan, or sell it to another person. This can work well for borrowers denied credit from the bank. Instead, the borrower strikes a deal directly with the seller. It's a win-win situation.

Interest rates matter

Interest is the cost of borrowing for the buyer and the reward for lending for the lender. As of the time of this writing, the interest rate on a 30-year fixed mortgage is around 4 percent. But back in 1981, it was over 18 percent.

Let's take our $205,000 loan from Hal as an example. If you borrowed this amount from a bank at 4 percent for a 30-year fixed loan, what you would actually pay back is $352,332. Just the cost of borrowing (not repaying the loan) would be $147,332. Now compare that with the same $205,000 over 30 years at 18 percent. Your total cost would be over a million dollars ($1,112,229), and interest alone would be $907,229.

One way of thinking about seller financing for the borrower is "rent to buy." Typically, a note will have a "balloon payment" within a few years. A balloon payment is repayment of the outstanding amount in one lump sum. The expectation is that the buyer will refinance the note at a lower interest rate in the future. Refinancing is a new loan that pays off the old loan. People refinance homes and businesses for one of two reasons: to get a lower rate on the new loan, or to get cash from equity (increase in value) of the asset.

Interest rates have been exceptionally low since the financial crash of 2007. However, if future interest rates skyrocket and a balloon payment is due, the buyer will be in for a nasty surprise. Yet it worked out well for us. After agreeing to repayment terms with Hal, we went down to see Hal's lawyer, filled out the paperwork, and moved into our first permanent location soon afterward.

Six months after moving into our new Critter Fixer 1 in Byron, we started work on Critter Fixer 2 in Bonaire, a suburb of Warner Robins. The iron was hot, and it was time to strike.

CHAPTER 5

Growth

In 2009, *Businessweek* 2named Warner Robins as the best place in Georgia to raise a family. But long before that, I knew growth was coming to nearby Warner Robins. Bonaire is two miles to the south of Warner Robins and a 30-minute drive from Fort Valley. We wanted to lease space in Bonaire for what was to become Critter Fixer 2. Back then, the only thing out there on Highway 96 was a liquor store, grocery store, and a McDonald's.

I read that a new McDonald's is an indicator of future growth. McDonald's has a very successful real estate division. Former CEO, Harry J. Sonneborn, was quoted as saying "We are not technically in the food business. We are in the real estate business." McDonald's buys land in up-and-coming areas. It sells the land where restaurants are underperforming. McDonald's also makes money by being a landlord to its franchisees, charging them a fee to use the McDonald's name, and selling them restaurant supplies.

Terrance and I could see the signs. Bonaire was expanding. It was building a new high school. New houses were going up. Businesses followed, and we wanted to be there. And we were right. Since 1990, Bonaire's population has more than doubled. Today, Warner Robins is booming.

We knew Mr. Bowles because he brought his dog to our Byron office. We learned he owned the property for lease in Bonaire. It was a liquor store with two additional leasable spaces on the side. But he wasn't interested in having a veterinarian hospital alongside his liquor store. He thought we would make too much noise with dogs barking.

I told him I'd rent both spaces. It was mostly bluff on my part. I was hoping he would say, "No that's okay, you can rent just the one." But to my dismay, he agreed. Uh-oh! Now it was time to put up or shut up. I paid for the whole thing out of earnings at Critter Fixer 1 in Byron and my wages from working nightshift at Macon Emergency Veterinarian Clinic. It was worth it because I could see the potential. Six months after opening our first clinic in Byron we opened Critter Fixer 2 in Bonaire in our newly leased space.

About a year and a half later, Mr. Bowles told us he was selling the liquor store. He asked me if I wanted to buy some land he owned to build a hospital. He owned acres and acres of land around the liquor store. We decided on a lot behind our current leased location. He thought enough of us to give us a low price. Today, that land is worth over 20 times what we paid for it. If you have a clothing store or a restaurant, you want to be facing the street. But for us, that didn't matter. You don't ride around with your dog and say:

Hmmm, since we're out, maybe I'll stop at the vet. We didn't mind not facing the street because Critter Fixer is a destination.

Good debt

By the time we came to buy the land from Mr. Bowles, the real estate value of Critter Fixer 1 in Byron had increased. We were paying down the loan to Hal Peavey. Now we owed less, and our building was worth more. We had equity; so we used our existing asset, Critter Fixer 1, as security to buy Mr. Bowles's land.

Leverage is simply borrowing money to invest it. Here's how it worked for us. Once we found how much Critter Fixer 1 was worth, we went to the bank and got a note with Critter Fixer 1 and the new property on it. We leveraged our existing asset. The bank gave us a $500,000 loan. It gave us that loan because we had proved ourselves as worthy business owners. We had a repayment history. Banks like that. And there was an increase in the value of the property we owned. We looked like a good bet.

In the previous chapter, I briefly noted there is good debt and bad debt. This was good debt because we took it on to boost future profits, and not to buy stuff, such as shoes, cars, and vacations which would be worth less later on. Our new debt allowed us to buy the land from Mr. Bowles and we paid off the balance owed to Hal Peavey. We used the remainder to build Critter Fixer 2.

I bought the land behind Mr. Bowles's liquor store in December 1999. We had to move only about 75 feet from the property we had been leasing into our new purpose-built clinic. We took six months to put up the building and move in.

When we built Critter Fixer 1, Hal's crew did most of the construction work. I worked with them and learned a lot. Hal was a licensed builder and Terrence and I did much of the labor. It was hard work, but for me, it was a great hands-on learning experience.

I hired an architect to draw up a plan for Critter Fixer 2. We hired a local builder to help with the new building. After working with Hal and watching our builder, it taught me I would never again need to hire another general contractor. I learned how to build from my observations and could handle anything we needed for future growth

Now we owned two properties and the business was thriving. But it wasn't without teething problems.

Learning to be boss

I had to learn how to be a good boss. It took about five years. Initially, I was only worried about keeping the lights on. Sometimes I would get angry and throw things across the room. Not surprisingly I had a problem with staff turnover. And it wasn't their fault. It was mine. I had to learn to control my anger because everything doesn't always go right. I could see opportunities, but they wouldn't work for me unless I managed myself better.

Misty was our first employee and receptionist at Critter Fixer 1. Melinda was our first employee at Critter Fixer 2. Misty and Melinda put up with a lot from me, because I hadn't yet learned to be a good boss. I wasn't setting myself up as a role model. Fortunately Melinda and Misty are forgiving and we remain friends to this day. Fire and brimstone, blame and accusations just don't work because people resent it. Sometimes I had to leave the room to control my anger. But eventually, I learned to become more patient with people and situations.

Most employees will do what they can get away with. That's just human nature. I learned never to embarrass an employee in front of other people. Nobody likes to be embarrassed. If I needed to criticize someone, I'd do it in my office. Every employee needs to be managed differently. And everyone deserves respect. A good boss shows them how they make a difference for good or bad to the success of the business and the whole team. I explained to them this is a young company and when I win you win.

Over time, I've invested in my employees. We have a bond. I tell them, "Everyone will eat good around here. If I eat good, so will my employees." Ask them and they will tell you. My employees work four days a week. Most own their own homes and those who aren't homeowners all stay in my rental properties. They're getting salaries they couldn't get any other place locally.

It's not that I get good employees. I develop them. I find people who are willing to learn and have a good attitude, and I teach them. You want your employees to become the people you need them to be. This is vitally important for a small company. A good boss nurtures, encourages, and teaches employees. It's all based on trust, respect, and care for their well-being. Only then they will be open to constructive criticism. We've all learned to understand each other. I used to be more volatile but not anymore. Even if I get mad it's over quickly.

Loyalty

Many of my employees have been with me for a long time, some for almost 20 years, and many over 10 years. Loyalty is how I've built my business. Your employees are the lifeblood of your business. They are in your innermost circle, at least for me they are anyway.

I've been burned by people I let into my circle. That's why it's important to have one or two, or maybe three circles. Your innermost circle allows you to sleep well at night. But people on the outer-most circle means that you may need to sleep with one eye open. Loyalty is a matter of degree. The more material wealth you have, the more people want to get to you. So you must surround yourself with people who truly are happy for your success, and know that if you are winning, the whole team is winning.

I've been fortunate enough to attend many major events, including the last six Super Bowls. My staff hasn't gone with me. Last year, before I headed to Houston to see my Atlanta Falcons play in the big game (still sickening to talk about it),

I counted out five one-hundred-dollar bills to each of my employees. I told them to have a good Super Bowl weekend.

I know I couldn't succeed without my dream team. Each one of them wants me to succeed. They understand their success depends on mine. We all want each other to win. When the hospital succeeds everyone gets bonuses. And I pay well. Ultimately my goal is to take care of my people, and they repay that with loyalty.

I'm loyal to my employees and they are to me. We have each other's backs. My employees know I have their best interests at heart. I expect a hundred percent, and they expect the same from me. Sometimes they do things wrong, but they know it's better to be chewed out than thrown out.

The business of business

When we started, I spent most of my time learning how to be a good veterinarian, but nothing about the business of business. If you're going to start a business, you must know your customers, what product or service you're offering— that they are willing to pay for—and why they should buy from you. For me, I had answered those questions. But I still had to learn about running a business. I hit the books.

If you're going to be a business owner, even before setting up your team, learn about what kind of business you're going to set up. Protect yourself from liabilities. What if someone trips over your doorstep and breaks their neck? What if you make a promise you can't keep, through no fault of your own? What if you make a mistake that costs your customer money? You can protect yourself through business structure and insurance.

Here is a brief overview of common business structures or "business entities." I'm not giving you legal advice so seek professional help. Nolo Press (nolo.com) is a good source for business legal information, do-it-yourself filing software, and easy-to-understand legal books. Another resource is legalzoom.com which provides online services for setting up your business.

Sole proprietor

The most common and simplest business entity is the sole proprietorship. This is a one-person business (although in one of the nine community property states the IRS will allow a qualified husband and wife to be treated as a sole proprietor.)

This is easy to set up. A sole proprietor does business as an individual. There is no distinction between the business and the owner. This means the owner is responsible for all taxes, profits, losses, and debts. And anything else that can go wrong. If someone wins a case against a sole proprietor, the business owner can lose house, car, and just about everything. You can see why a sole proprietor should be careful and buy general liability insurance. Commercial general liability (CGL) is a standard policy for businesses against liability for bodily injury, property damage, advertising injury, operations, and personal injury. Even with insurance, you must act responsibly.

In Georgia, there is no need to file papers with the Georgia Secretary of State when establishing a sole proprietorship. Choose a business name. If your business name isn't your own name, file a "trade name" with the Clerk of the Superior Court. You may need a business license from your city, and any special licenses, for example, if you're opening a hair salon. If you sell directly to the public, you will probably have to collect sales tax and pass that along to the State. You must keep records.

Even though there is no distinction between business and personal liability, a sole proprietor should separate personal and business expenses, because business expenses are tax-deductible, and personal ones are not. It's a good idea to open a separate bank account in the business name. You can get a free Employer Identification Number (EIN) for your business from the IRS. For a sole proprietor, your EIN is linked to your Social Security Number (SSN). You'll be expected to estimate and pay taxes every three months, and pay self-employment tax which covers Social Security contributions.

Partnership

Be careful what you sign. A friend from college approached me with a business idea. I'll call him Ken. He planned to start a car dealership. I looked at the lot. His idea sounded good, so I put up most of the money. A year-and-a-half later he was prospering.

A "general partnership" is easy to set up. The problem is it's risky because partners have unlimited liability. And it gets worse because a single partner can act on behalf of the partnership. Without separation of personal and business assets, one partner can expose the other to personal liability. If one partner does something stupid, the other partners are on the hook for the consequences. And that's what happened to me.

Trust but verify

One day, I'm in my clinic and a woman comes in with a bulldog. She was a very nice lady.

She says, "Dr. Hodges, I've been trying to reach you for a week. The only way I could get to talk to you was to bring in this dog."

"What's wrong with your dog?"

She says, "Nothing." She pulls out some documents. "Your name is on this paperwork guaranteeing a line of credit."

Sure enough, my name was on that document as Ken's silent partner.

"This line of credit is in default. We're picking up all the cars right now. You are responsible for paying all the delinquencies."

I had heard about Ken's shady business dealings sometime before. As soon as I did, I told Ken to take me off the paperwork. So this visit to my clinic was a surprise. I thought I had already disassociated myself entirely from any business responsibilities. I remember telling Ken my name is more important than anything. I thought I had done enough by telling him to remove my name, and I walked away. But I was wrong.

Nobody's perfect. I've learned that occasionally good people do bad things, but if they continue to do bad things, that's just the way they are. Ken was using the business line of credit for personal expenditures and selling cars not paid for. If you've worked for a company as an employee almost all your life, and now you become the owner, you can be dazzled by the bright lights, and think you're the man. Despite my constant pleading to listen to me with my years of experience as a business owner, when the checks started rolling in, he felt he knew it all.

I did have my name on paperwork showing I was no longer part of the company, but I didn't follow up to make sure I was taken off the lines of credit. My name was still on those. It cost me over $100,000 to clear my name, a painful lesson. Ken was sued, I was sued, and the company was sued. I had to go to court.

Sitting in front of that jury was embarrassing. Prosecutors and defense attorneys look for impartial jurors. But that's tough in a small community. I'm well-known. I'm on TV. I sit on several boards. I'm known for positive work I've done over the last 20 years. Because of this, I've earned the benefit of the doubt in my community.

It was impossible to find all twelve people to have never heard of me. Fortunately, they had only heard of me in a positive light. Some even came up to me after the trial and gave me a hug, thanking me for my community support. Many said how glad they were that Ken admitted to his wrongdoing. The case against me was dismissed.

It was a humbling experience sitting there being judged by a jury of your peers. I'm thankful Ken finally admitted to his mistakes. He pleaded guilty and has to pay for his wrongdoing. I'm not bitter. I believe Ken learned from his mistakes. I learned my lesson about who I associate with. Each of us can make mistakes when judging character. My lesson as far as character goes is trust but verify. The business lesson: I needed a better business structure than a general partnership.

A limited partnership (LLP) is another entity which offers protection for all members except the managing partner. If Ken and I had chosen an LLP, he would have been liable because he would have been the active managing partner; my liability would have been limited. For an LLP, the managing partner is exposed to personal liability, but other partners are protected, as long as they don't actively manage the business.

Limited Liability Company (LLC)

An LLC is popular with entrepreneurs and real estate investors. It's a relatively new business entity. It became available in Wyoming in 1977 but most states didn't follow until the 1990s. An LLC is easy to start and has fewer legal requirements than setting up a corporation. But there are more startup costs than a sole proprietorship. An LLC is governed by the laws of your state, giving you a lot of flexibility. You register your LLC with your Secretary of State.

The beauty of an LLC is it separates the business from the business owner(s). You get protection for your personal assets if something goes wrong. It's the business that gets sued, not you. The owners of an LLC are called members. LLCs can have unlimited members, but an S corporation (which I'll talk about in just a minute) limits the number of its shareholders. LLCs have members; corporations have shareholders.

It's possible to have a single-member LLC, but generally, LLCs have more than one member. LLC members create an "operating agreement" which outlines how the company will be run and its ownership.

An LLC raises money to invest in the business through its members. For example, let's say four founder members get together to form their limited liability company. Each member initially contributes $10,000, so each has a 25 percent "interest" (ownership) in the new company.

Corporation

Critter Fixer is an S corporation. The S corporation is a special business structure which became available in 1958. It has more requirements than the newer LLC, but there are many similarities. Both S corporations and LLCs separate the business from the owners (members/shareholders), offer limited liability protection, and are subject to state requirements.

Both S corporations and LLCs must file a separate business tax return (except for a single-member LLC). Only U.S. citizens or permanent residents can be shareholders of an S corporation. What makes S corporations and LLCs attractive is "pass-through taxation." This means there is no federal corporate tax. Instead, the tax is "passed through" and paid on any profits the shareholders' or members' have on their federal individual tax returns. State tax is another story. You'll need to check the rules for your state. A good place to start is your secretary of state's website.

Members in an LLC can manage themselves if they choose. This is why members write an operating agreement to say who does what, and how the company will be run. An S corporation has more rules. It has a board of directors which oversees major decisions, but board members are not involved in the day-to-day running of the business. Instead, the board elects officers to manage operations. When it comes time to sell your S corporation, you'll find the process easier as long as you play by the IRS rules. Shares in an S corporation are freely transferable, but an LLC requires the approval of other members to sell. This is by no means an exhaustive list of differences.

Most big business is structured through a C corporation. C corporations can be owned by anyone, even other corporations. When you buy a share in a company you own a tiny slice. The biggest difference between a traditional C corporation and an S corporation is how they are taxed. C corporations are taxed twice, once at the corporate level, and once at the individual level. But both offer liability protection. And protecting your business is a big deal, no matter how you structure it.

I learned about insurance in the sauna.

Hot talk

I was at my gym. Next to me in the sauna was a gentleman named Andy Thomas. We got to talking. I learned he was starting his own insurance business. Now Andy is my go-to guy for insurance. He holds over 75 policies for me.

Tax guy

I found my tax guy right next to the little paint shop in Byron: Smallwood Accounting. You need someone to keep you on the straight and narrow, especially with taxes. Rick Smallwood is my guy. He has kept me out of tax troubles for the last 20 years. Learn your tax responsibilities. A business owner is responsible for withholding and paying employee payroll taxes; Workmen's Compensation taxes, paying half employee Social Security contributions, and in several states, disability insurance. Every month we have to deposit our collected sales tax with the state. A good accountant will save you time, money, and help you stay out of trouble. The good news is accountants will not only simplify things for you, but save you money in taxes, and you can deduct what you pay them.

Being nice

When we were boys in the Trap, there were lookouts to watch out for trouble. Businesses need lookouts too. In my practice, I see drug reps because I buy a lot of drugs (legal ones). I spend between $50,000 and $60,000 a month on drugs. Right from the start of Critter Fixer 1, we were always pleasant to sales representatives. They tell me some doctors make them wait for an hour, and then only give them a few minutes of their time. When I meet people I try to form relationships beneficial for both of us.

Some of my biggest allies are drug representatives. When we moved from the back of the liquor store into our new Critter Fixer 2, a drug representative came and helped us move. Drug representatives became our lookouts. They are our eyes and ears. We got to hear what some people were saying about us. We heard from one rep that a fellow vet in Warner Robins was saying those two black guys would never make it beyond a year.

I proved him wrong.

Our veterinarian practice is thriving today. I love being a vet. I love saving lives.

I always go to continuing education classes and learn the latest vet techniques. But I also enjoy learning about becoming an entrepreneur, and how to develop multiple streams of income.

PART II

CHAPTER 6

First adventures in real estate

(2004-2008)

I taught myself to buy real estate by reading books. I realized that I didn't need to be limited to being a vet. When I came across *Multiple Streams of Income* by Robert Allen, it got me excited. Mr. Allen spent over twenty years working with successful people. *Multiple Streams of Income* is an idea book. It opened my eyes to new possibilities. And that's just what I was looking for, ideas on how I could diversify my income. I wanted to find other businesses that would bring in regular income.

My first opportunity as a real estate investor came through a chance to help my good friend and fraternity brother, Earnest Harvey. He was a schoolteacher from Cordele, a poor community where 41.6 percent of the population is below the poverty line. Earnest wanted to move to Warner Robins and he needed a place to stay. I told him how much homes in Warner Robins were.

"Man, I don't know if I can afford it," he said.

I said, "I've always wanted to buy real estate. How about if I find a house, and fix it up, would you be willing to move in?"

He said, "Sure."

When I bought my first rental house in 2004, I already had Earnest ready to rent.

I paid $60,000 for the house and put in another $10,000 for construction costs. I've always been interested in building things, and this first house turned out to be a great investment. Earnest and his family rented from me for six years, and I still have that property. I was encouraged so I bought other houses. But it wasn't all gravy.

Beginner's mistakes

That same year of 2004, I bought a duplex for $16,000 in Macon. I found the listing in the local newspaper. What a deal! I figured I'd make a killing. But I didn't have the money for a down payment, so I talked to the people at the bank and secured a line of credit. But I was nervous. I kept going back and looking at the building. I took a week to pull the trigger.

One side of the duplex was in good shape. The other one wasn't. I remodeled the building. Even though it looked like a great investment on paper, it turned out to be lousy.

The problem was the neighborhood. My new building was in a rough area, right across from a housing project on Houston Road in Macon. I got to know a few people who lived in the neighborhood, but it was scary. It was so scary I didn't want to be there after dark.

Mistake number one was not paying attention to the location. Real estate value depends on three important elements: location, location, location. Never buy a property you wouldn't feel comfortable going to at night.

Mistake number two was not paying attention to my potential renter's history. If someone had the money and wanted to rent from me, I was like, okay, as long as you have your deposit, I'll rent to you. I hadn't yet learned to do background checks.

One day I got a call from the District Attorney's Office in Detroit. The caller said they needed to find a place for a person and would pay the first year's rent. That sounded good. I was super happy when that check arrived. But this person was in a year-long witness protection program. After the year was over he wouldn't pay.

I still hadn't learned my lesson about location. I bought another house for $14,000 right around the corner in the Hood. My renter was a woman with many kids. But then she went missing. She just disappeared. The police called and said the young kids were in the house alone. I had to help figure out a solution. Her children went to live with their grandparents. As far as I know, she was never found.

I sold all the headaches.

I didn't make a profit, but I got back close to what I paid for the properties. The big lesson for me was, don't buy the right house in the wrong neighborhood. Later, I turned this on its head by buying an eyesore in the right neighborhood. And that's a whole different story with a much better outcome. I'll tell you about that in Chapter 8.

Reading

I learned about what money is, and what it isn't, from *Multiple Streams of Income*. But parts of the book are no longer current. For example, Mr. Allen writes about the power of compound interest: how money makes money all by itself.

Back in 2005 when this book came out, you could double your money in a 6 percent savings account in about 12 years. Compare that with what banks offer savers at the time of writing this book: 0.86 percent. That means you would need to wait 84 years to double your money. You're not going to get rich, even slowly, by putting your money in a savings account. That doesn't mean that a savings account has no value. Everyone needs an emergency fund.

But low interest isn't the only downside to a savings account. There is inflation: how your money loses buying power over time. If you ever saw some of those old movies where a cup of coffee cost a dime, you'll know what I mean.

A dime doesn't get you much today. And then there are taxes. So, doubling the buying power of your money in a "safe" investment will never happen at low-interest rates.

Multiple Streams of Income is not a get-rich-quick book, but it does lay out important financial principles. The essential idea is cash flow; the money flowing into and out of your business monthly. If more money is coming into your business than is going out, you have positive cash flow. That's good. And cash flow is what rental investing is all about. If your bills exceed your income, you have negative cash flow. If this goes on for long you're likely to go out of business. The Small Business Administration says that lack of cash is a top reason businesses fail. You want a predictable stream of income, but you must be patient.

When you put a peach pit in the ground it takes a long time for it to grow into a tree. Only then you'll harvest your peaches—if bugs or bad weather doesn't ruin them. Likewise, investments usually take a long time to show a profit. In the beginning, most businesses don't have positive cash flow. Even though the business may be making money, startup expenses (equipment, payroll, tax, land, etc.) eat up your profit.

Here's an example. Imagine you will make ice cream and sell it. You have to learn how to make it, buy your equipment and supplies. You must advertise because it doesn't matter how delicious your ice cream is if no one knows where to find it. You do all this before you've made $1 in profit. And that dollar doesn't go in your pocket. It goes to paying down what you owe to set yourself up in business: startup costs. Initially, you can expect to have negative cash flow. But don't let it go on too long.

Watch your cash flow, because how you manage your money is the difference between long-term wealth and bankruptcy. According to experts at the National Endowment for Financial Education, most people who win the lottery go broke within just a few years. If you can't manage what you have now, you probably can't manage greater wealth, at least not on your own.

A team of advisers can help, but reading works well, and learning the basics of how to manage your money is betting on yourself. The problem is children in school don't learn about money, and most adults have never gone to personal-finance class. Yet learning how to make money—and how to handle it—have a lot to do with the quality of your life. A major principle of building wealth is simple: spend less than you make.

Moving up

My next foray into real estate investing was to buy a fixer-upper in a better neighborhood. I did some of the remodeling work myself. Construction is a good trade to learn. I could paint, hammer, and put up sheetrock. I hired two other guys. I learned that if you treat people with respect they'll do just about anything for you. Candyman was an older guy and an excellent woodworker. But he was practically homeless. Sometimes he stayed with one of his friends. But when he had no place to go, I let him stay in the house while we were fixing it up. My original tenant is still there all these years later. It's been a good investment.

I then bought a four-bedroom house on Cox Drive. The property is in an affordable Warner Robins neighborhood with a good location, right across the street from a school playground. My long-term tenant is also one of my Critter Fixer employees. What gives me joy is that I'm providing affordable and quality housing for people who wouldn't otherwise get it.

The good, bad, and the ugly

All successful businesses solve a problem. The problem I'm solving is to turn the bad and the ugly into the good; so it's an affordable, fine, and decent place to live. And that increases value for the renter and the owner.

As an investor, I want to buy a wreck, fix it up myself, and then rent it out. I don't want to buy captivating. I want ugly. And I want it cheap. I trained my realtor, Stacy, to become an investor's realtor. I look for opportunity and potential, not what the typical home buyer wants. They want "impeccable" and "luxurious". Or at least those two words in real estate ads attract home buyers.

Let's look at some similarities and differences between retail home buyers and investors. Both groups will pay more for a property in a good neighborhood with good schools. This is because property values are likely to increase.

Retail home buyers and investors need cash, or good credit to get a loan. If homebuyers don't have good credit, they may be lucky and buy a home where the owner will loan them money (at higher interest rates). This is how I purchased the first Critter Fixer property from Hal Peavey (Chapter 4). The owner will use the property as security. So, if the borrower fails to pay, the property goes back to the owner. Ouch!

A home for yourself

Stacy was always a fine agent for people looking for the American Dream of homeownership. Her clients want to buy a home in move-in condition. They want freshly painted walls, solid construction, with good flooring. But buying a home to live in is unlikely to build wealth, at least not in the way rental property can.

Yes, buying a house to live in will probably increase in value. But if you sell it, you still need a place to live. And it's likely the house you want to buy will be the same price or more expensive than the one you sold.

When you price in all your costs, such as repairs, transaction fees, and interest on your loans, you may not come out ahead. To build wealth, you'll be better off buying rental property. When you're starting out, and you insist on buying your own home, buy a duplex. Live in one side, and rent out the other side.

Let's start with the basics. Imagine for a moment you're a usual homebuyer and not a real estate investor. You just want to buy a home to live in it. Here are the normal steps for a retail buyer.

Figure out how much house you can afford. There are online calculators to help you with this one. A rule of thumb is two-and-a-half times your before-tax salary. If you make $36,000 you can probably buy a house costing $90,000.

Next, find money for your down payment and closing costs. Typically lenders want 20 percent down. So, if the house costs $90,000, you need $18,000 for a down payment. But it doesn't stop there. You'll need more money for closing costs. These are fees to have the property appraised by an appraiser, title searches by title companies to ensure that you really will be the legal owner and are buying the property from a legitimate owner. Taxes, credit report charges, deed-recording fees, and more are all part of closing costs. Closing costs can run from two to five percent of the purchase price. Your realtor should give you a "buyer's net sheet" which explains all these fees.

The seller pays the realtor's fees, the buyer doesn't.

Now is the time to apply for a preapproved loan. Once you've determined your budget, find a lender, usually a bank or credit union.

Next, look at different mortgages. Fair lending is required by law. Get information from several lenders. A mortgage is negotiable; the interest rate you'll pay depends on the length of your mortgage and your credit score: shop, compare, and negotiate.

You may be tempted to get an adjustable-rate mortgage (ARM) with low payments now, but higher payments later. Usually, this only works if you will live in the house for a short period, about five years, or until the payments ratchet upward, or a balloon payment is due.

Many people were holding adjustable-rate mortgages during the subprime mortgage crisis of 2007-2010. The causes of that crisis are too complex to go into in this book, but banks had sold mortgages to people who couldn't afford them. When they couldn't pay their loans, home prices collapsed. Many people went bankrupt and lost everything. A more predictable mortgage is the standard 30-year fixed-rate mortgage. Other people prefer a 15-year fixed-rate mortgage. There are a lot of variables.

Next, you'll want to find a real estate agent that's right for you. As I've said before, relationships matter. Ask around. Find someone you can trust. An experienced realtor will know the right questions to ask. She'll be well connected to a network of other professionals. She'll know the neighborhoods.

Which neighborhoods attract you? Why? How many bedrooms do you need? How many bathrooms? How close to school do you want to be? These are just a few questions to ask yourself before you go looking for properties.

While you're looking for the right house, shop around for home-owner insurance. And when you've found a house you want to buy, have it inspected for defects, and then put in an offer. If the seller accepts your offer, review the contract carefully. Before signing, have enough cash to cover all the expenses. Once you sign, the property is yours.

So, that's how to buy a house to live in. How does real estate investing work?

A home for somebody else

Some people buy houses, fix them up, and resell them at a profit. But that's not what I'm doing. I'm in it for the long term. Value for me is cash flow from rents. I want to keep the houses I buy. Properties will increase in value over time and add to my wealth. The beauty of it is I'm not paying my mortgages: my renters are.

As the rental property increases in value and interest rates are low, I can refinance. This means I can base a larger loan on the new value of the property. Then I can use that money for down payments to buy more properties. Banks like this because they make money charging refinancing fees. They also like it because the loans are secured by the properties you buy, and your renters will be paying off the loan in predictable installments.

When you buy a home for yourself, the loan amount is based on your personal earnings. But you can buy a more valuable rental property (even if it's in bad shape) because that loan will generate cash flow from rental income. A home of your own doesn't generate cash unless you refinance. Even then, you're borrowing money. Building wealth depends on what you do with the cash you take out. The advantage of rental property is that it generates cash, pays down the loan, and adds to your net worth.

Net worth is your wealth: what you own, less what you owe. Net worth is assets minus liabilities (debts). According to a study by Pew Research Center, the median household net worth for black households in 2013 was $11,200. The median is the midpoint, so there were as many African Americans with net worth below $11,200 than above it. I'll have more to say about managing money in Chapter 11: Money 101.

Foreclosure is when the bank takes back possession of a mortgaged property when the homeowner fails to keep up with mortgage payments. If the terms of the loan are in default, the lender may demand full payment. Most people can't come up with such a big chunk of money, so they're forced to sell the property. And those properties can be picked up at auction for much less than market value.

I always look for a deal. Many properties I buy are in foreclosure. Sometimes people sell a property quickly due to some life event, for example, job loss, or when the owner has passed away. People leave behind all kinds of personal effects, books, and interesting artifacts. In one attic I found a cool Christmas tree with red lights. I think about who lived there and what their lives were like.

The next thing I did was to buy a brick house on Dewey Street in Warner Robins. It's a good house and has doubled in value since.

My realtor doesn't like it

Then I bought a house against the judgment of my real estate agent. It was across town in one of the better neighborhoods. When I first went to see it, I opened the door and immediately saw the problem: evidence of flooding. A foot off the floor was a water line. It may have been flooded on purpose because the previous occupant had left behind a lot of stuff.

The realtor told me not to buy it because of mold. Mold is a scary thing in the housing business. I didn't see any mold. I assumed there was some. I bought the house anyway.

But this problem/opportunity forced me to ask myself serious questions. Could I go from just making minor cosmetic changes to serious remodeling? Could I replace sheetrock throughout the house? I had guys who could do that. So, we tore up all the flooring, cut the sheetrock out, and remodeled the house.

I bought this asset for $50,000 and I put another $10,000 into remodeling costs. By the time we finished it was worth $130,000. But I wasn't about to sell it. It became my first flagship rental house. A flagship house is in the best neighborhood with best schools. This was the first time I charged a "high-cotton" rent. Rents are significantly higher on this side of town. I still own the property today and my tenant is a school principal.

Three years after buying my first rental, I had a team: a realtor, banker, insurance, and construction people. Andy Thomas is my insurance guy. I learned that you shouldn't go to the bank when you need money. Build the relationship first. Mac Harden was my banking mentor. Earlier he'd helped me buy the second Critter Fixer. I'll have more to say about him in the next chapter.

I learned about the importance of location and checking renters' backgrounds. I could now assess whether a property was worth buying within about twenty minutes of seeing it.

I'd boosted my construction skills, but I was becoming a better big-picture guy. I saw how everything fit together.

In late 2006, I took a break from buying real estate. I wanted to learn how to trade stocks. I did well at first. How was I to know that on September 29, 2008, the stock market would take a nose dive?

CHAPTER 7

Buy low, sell high

It was like taking candy from a baby. At the push of a button, I was making big money in the stock market. This was so much easier than buying rental properties. I was a genius!

Making money in the stock market is simple. Buy low, sell high. I learned that much in the Trap. But there's a big difference in knowing what to do, and actually doing it. Buy low, sell high is easy to understand, but difficult to do consistently. But I hadn't learned that yet. I didn't realize that it just wasn't me picking winning stocks. Almost all stocks were rising in early 2008. Or, as the saying goes: all boats rise on an incoming tide.

Maybe I'm getting ahead of myself, so let me explain what the stock market is and how I got into it. Initially, I knew little. I read and learned as I went along.

People in my community ask me how to make money in the stock market. Before I go into details, I want to know they have at least helped themselves. I ask them, what is the Dow? What is a ticker symbol? I ask them what they have read. If they know nothing, I tell them to find a book, answer those questions and come back. Sadly, few do. Just like real estate investing, I taught myself about the stock market.

When I was growing up I knew nobody who understood anything about the stock market. If you know nothing about the market, here are a few basics, and the story of what happened to me. You can make money, a lot of money, but you can also lose your shirt.

What is the stock market?

Swap meets and yard sales are marketplaces where buyers and sellers come together to trade. The stock market is not much different. The term stock market covers a whole range of trading exchanges around the world where public companies are listed. As a stock investor, you want to buy shares (also called, equities, stocks, or securities), hold them for a while, wait till the price goes up, and sell them at a profit.

Buy low, sell high.

A news story can send stocks skyward or plummetting. Investing in stocks is risky, but there is no reward without risk. There are no guarantees, so don't invest in the stock market with money you'll need in the next two to five years.

That's because stock prices can rise and fall dramatically over short periods of time.

The odds are stacked against gamblers. In the casino, the house always wins. In the stock market, there are two sides to every transaction: buyers and sellers, winners and losers. If the stock market were a person, he would be bi-polar. Greed and fear run the stock market. Stock prices are random over the short term. But over the long term, over 10 or 15 years, these fitful ups and downs have a history of evening out.

A piece of the action

When you buy shares, even one share, in a public company you're buying a part of that company. You own part of that company. You may even go to an annual shareholder meeting and vote on who is running the organization.

What makes a company private is that its ownership is not open to the public. A private company can be a mom-and-pop store, or a large corporation such as a supermarket chain like Albertsons. Private companies don't sell shares on the stock market.

Public companies issue shares that can be bought and sold in the stock market. Public companies have thousands or millions of shares outstanding. That means the company's ownership is divided into many slices or fractions owned by investors (you), institutions, other companies, or for sale by brokers.

At one time only the rich were clients of expensive stockbrokers who bought and sold shares on their behalf. These transactions were done by phone or face-to-face. Some still are done that way today. But most transactions are done online right on your computer or smartphone. Today with online trading, anyone can participate. Anyone can own part of a public company. Stocks and other financial products are bought and sold through a "brokerage" account at a financial service company such as E*TRADE or Fidelity Investments.

You need a brokerage account to buy and sell stocks. TD Ameritrade has no account minimum, but their commissions are $6.95 per trade, and you must put money in that account if you want to buy and sell. At Charles Schwab, you'll need $1000 to start, but their commissions are $4.95 per trade.

Brokerage commissions for buying and selling shares have come way down recently. And they will probably have changed by the time you read this book. Whether you buy 10 shares or 10,000, the commission is $4.95.

Hidden costs

Besides commissions, there are other costs called the spread or bid-ask price. This is the difference between the broker's buying price and the selling price: the brokerage company pockets the difference. There's not much you can do about this because prices and spreads are constantly changing. Whether you sell or buy, the investment company always makes money in commissions and spreads.

Volume is the number of shares of a company traded in a single day. The number of shares traded affects the bid-ask price.

Here is why volume affects the spread and your costs of buying and selling. Imagine there are two toll bridges. One is in a busy location (high volume), and another one gets little traffic (low volume). The toll for the high-traffic bridge is low because many vehicles are paying for the bridge upkeep. Let's say each vehicle pays $1. But each vehicle crossing the low-traffic bridge must pay more (say, $4) to generate the same money. This is why a heavily traded stock is likely to have a low spread such as a fraction of a penny. That means more of your money goes to buy your shares and less goes to the broker. Brokers charge less because they'll make it up in volume.

Companies are identified by a ticker symbol. McDonald's is MCD. This company trades over three million shares each day. Back in 2008, that was over ten million shares a day. So McDonald's is not as popular today than it was. When vast numbers of shares are changing hands every second, you can see how just a fraction of a penny in the spread adds up to big money for the investment company.

Fifty years ago the average holding period for a stock was eight years. Today that average is around five days. Many people hold onto stocks for decades, but there are computers trading with computers many times a second. Prices vary throughout the trading day. No one person can understand all the factors that affect the value or price of the stock. Stocks are risky, but some are riskier than others.

I take risks, but they're educated risks. My advice is to think about what you're good at and what you're passionate about. And that means being willing to invest the time to learn. Because we don't all start out being good at whatever we do.

Every time a stock trades the brokerage company makes money. High volume also means there are active buyers and sellers. There are people willing to buy what you sell. This is called liquidity. Popular stocks are liquid. You can turn them around in a second or two because there are always buyers for what you're selling.

On the other hand, low volume/high spread means you are paying more for ownership. But the real problem is when you come to sell. If your broker can't find buyers, then your stock is illiquid. Some stocks go to zero when no one wants them.

Good news for young investors

Almost everybody needs to have some part of their wealth in stocks. Historically, investing in stocks has been an effective long-term bet. This is good news for young investors. Time is on your side. If you regularly add to your investments when the market is up—and when it's down, you're likely to do better than traders who jump in and out of stocks. Investors plan to get rich slowly.

Day traders often buy and sell the same stock many times on the same day. I made $150,000 in just one day. And I've lost $89,000 in one day, too. Traders look to make a quick killing and get out. Investors usually win over the long term. But successful investing requires understanding, discipline, and patience. But there is a less risky and easier way. I'll get to that in a moment.

Excitement is the problem

At the end of 2007, E*TRADE was advertising heavily. I set up an account. I put in $90,000. A year later that money had grown to $1.5 million. It was so exciting. I was in a state of euphoria. I was chasing hot stocks. Priceline.com (PCLN) was the first stock I bought. I bought Amazon (AMZN) and Apple (AAPL) and others. They kept going up, and then they went up more!

I woke up every morning and watched CNBC. I still recommend watching this channel. And I continue to subscribe to the Wall Street Journal and other financial news sources. I learned the terminology. When I had a few minutes between patients at Critter Fixer, I'd go into the back of my office and trade stocks. It was fun. It was exciting. Exciting was the problem. I knew just enough to be dangerous.

Buying and selling online

The simplest order is called a market order. You click the choice that says market, and your order will execute instantaneously at the next price. That means you bought it.

But what price did you get? Go to your orders screen to check. Let's imagine your real-time stock quote is $10.25. But a second later it has gone up to $10.28. You just bought at a more expensive price.

Or, if you're trying to sell, the quote is $10.25, but everyone else is selling. A second later that stock has dropped to $10.20, or worse. Now you sold stock at a price cheaper than you wanted.

When buying a stock you can choose a limit order. This means you specify the price you're willing to pay. I'll use the same example: $10.25. You can put a limit order in for any price. If you think that the stock is too high-priced right now, you could put a limit order in to buy at $10.20. Then only if the asking price drops to $10.20 (even for a fraction of a second) will your order turn into a market order and execute.

I didn't know about stop loss. But I learned the hard way. You can use a stop loss order to limit your losses. If the stock drops beyond the price you specify, the stop loss will kick in and sell at the market price. Yes, you will lose, but you limit your losses.

If you bought the stock at $10.25, and you put in a stop loss order for $9.25, you know that worst case scenario, you will lose approximately one dollar per share. That's going to be painful, but not as painful as when you wake up, turn on your computer, and realize it's now only worth $0.10. It could happen. I put a stop loss on stocks at 20 percent below what I bought them for. If another crash occurs, my losses will be limited.

Not long after I started trading, E*TRADE offered me a margin account. They extended credit so I could buy more. Now I was able to buy five times the amount of stocks. Before I knew it, my margin account was over $2.5 million. It never crossed my mind that if it's too good to be true, then it is too good to be true.

A margin account is risky. I said earlier, leverage is borrowing money to invest. It amplifies gains, and losses. With a regular "cash account" you can lose all the money you invest. That's the worst case. But with a margin account, you can lose much more than you invest.

Think of it this way. You give me $10 to gamble for you. The gamble doesn't pay off. You're out $10. But what if you leverage your $10 as a down payment to borrow $90? Now you have a $90 stake. If you win, you win big. But what if you lose? You're out your own $10 plus the $90 you borrowed.

With a margin account, you pay what you borrowed plus some interest. The smart money says people new to investing should steer clear of margin accounts. I didn't know that.

Crash

On Monday, September 29, 2008, the stock market took a nosedive. The Dow suffered its biggest one-day decline, ever. The Dow Jones Industrial Average (DJIA) commonly known as "the Dow" is an important index of 30 companies traded on the New York Stock Exchange (NYSE). It's often called an indicator of the overall market performance, even though it's only 30 companies.

Investors were selling like crazy.

I'd seen nothing like it. My ego got in the way. I made a bet on MasterCard and Goldman Sachs. As the market was plummeting I believed these prices would come back. But I was throwing good money after bad. As the prices went down, I bought more. Instead of going back up, those stock prices kept falling. There's a saying in the stock market: don't catch a falling knife. But that's what I was doing. I lost a little over $1,000,000.

I lost more than my own money because I bought on margin. I stopped looking at the financial news and my portfolio, it was too depressing. My losses were mounting. I use my emergency fund to pay off all the money I owed for my margin account. I had lost my fortune.

Getting back to even

Looking back, the crash taught me to be stronger. I learned not to be afraid, and to believe in myself. I kept reading. I came across Jim Cramer's book, *Getting Back to Even*. I regularly watched his show on CNBC, Mad Money.

Cramer defines Mad Money as money to invest in stocks, not money you'll need for retirement. Until the crash, he'd been giving advice on individual stocks, and he still does today. But the crash in 2008 changed his perspective. Today, Mad Money is still an entertaining show, and it intends to educate viewers about money and the stock market.

Asset mix

Stocks are one asset class. Bonds, cash, real estate, precious metals are other asset classes. A bond is a type of IOU. When you buy a bond you are loaning your money to the issuer of the bond; a corporation or government. They use that money to expand operations. In return, you earn interest for the life of the bond, and then you get back what you paid for it. In general, you earn a higher interest on a ten-year bond than you would on a two-year bond. You can trade bonds and other debt instruments, but that's beyond the scope of this book. I'm just covering basics here.

The most common asset classes for ordinary investors are stocks and bonds. Cramer always suggests you do your homework. And you need to understand a lot when buying individual stocks. It's almost a full-time job. Anything else is gambling. Gambling on the stock market is not a reliable way to build wealth. But it is sure is thrilling – until you lose your shirt.

Mutual funds are a portfolio (a collection) of stocks, or bonds, or a mix of stocks and bonds. With a mutual fund, you get diversification. When you own a group of stocks (being diversified), you're lowering your risk. Some will do well, and others will crash and burn. Instead of buying a few individual stocks, mutual funds allow you to spread your risk.

Over the long term, your wealth is more dependent on the mix of assets you choose, rather than individual stock picks. That's because when stocks are down, bonds tend to go up. Different sectors of the economy, such as energy, technology, or commercial real estate, behave differently. One may be doing well while another is in trouble. A good mix of assets tends to even things out.

Mutual funds have a ticker symbol, just like stocks do. Each investor owns shares in the mutual fund. The mutual fund invests in a portfolio of stocks/bonds. You can buy a professionally managed fund. An active fund is where fund managers choose what and when to buy and sell. The mutual fund company will do the research and make buy/sell decisions, so you don't have to. If a mutual fund trades a lot, it will incur more costs than one that doesn't trade often.

But many studies have shown that active funds don't beat the market in the long run. Enter low-cost, passive investing: indexing.

Buy everything

So it was at this point I learned about index funds. Instead of picking individual winners and losers, the index fund seeks to own a portion of all of the stocks in the index. So, for an index of the U.S. stock market, if the whole market goes up, or down, so will the value of your investments. And over time that has been a very good bet.

Active fund managers look to beat the market. There are exceptions, but this has proved very difficult to do in the long run. When you buy an index fund you're getting exposure to all stocks in that index. There are several indexes. You can buy an index of the entire U.S. stock market, the U.S. bond market, foreign country stocks or bonds. You can even by an index of segments of the U.S. market, such as industrial stocks, or healthcare stocks.

You can buy mutual funds directly from companies such as The Vanguard Group which has the largest family of mutual funds. You can also buy mutual funds through an online stock brokerage account.

When you buy and sell an individual stock, you're charged a fee. But what if you're constantly trading? Those prices add up.

For an investor just starting, index funds can lower your risk and save you money. For example, an investor with $3000 can buy The Vanguard Total Market Stock Index Fund (VTSMX). After that, you can add to your investment in any amount over $1 at no transaction fee. This fund charges 0.15 percent a year. That means $7.50 a year on a balance of $5,000. If you have as much as $10,000 to invest, you can buy their Admiral shares (VTSAX) in the same fund at just 0.04 percent.

Slow and steady

Day trading is exciting. Watching a mutual fund gain a few cents is about as exciting as watching paint dry. Thinking about the difference between day traders, who can win big and lose big, and long-term investors reminds me of the fable about the tortoise and the hare.

In this story, the hare mocks the tortoise for being so slow.

"How will you ever get to your destination?" says the hare.

The tortoise replies, "Don't you worry, I'll get there in the end."

The tortoise is not to be dissed, so he challenges the hare to a race. The hare thinks: How could this tortoise beat a fast rabbit-like creature like me? The hare laughs at the ridiculousness of the idea but agrees to the challenge. A fox, who is watching all this, agrees to act as judge. They mark out the course, and off they go.

The hare speeds ahead. The tortoise is far behind. The tortoise thinks: This challenge wasn't such a good idea after all. But he keeps going.

After a while, the hare looks around and sees the tortoise way behind in the distance. And clearly he's much faster than the tortoise, so he takes a nap. But the tortoise keeps going. When the hare finally wakes up from his nap, he sees the tortoise ahead of him just about to cross the finish line. No matter how fast the hare can run he can't catch up.

So the moral of the story is slow and steady wins the race. And this is true of investing, too.

You can make investing a habit. It's easy to do. Using a mutual fund you can invest a portion of your pay regularly. Dollar cost averaging is a method where you decide how much you want to invest, each week or month or whatever, no matter how the market is doing. When the market is up, you will buy fewer shares. When the market is down, you buy more shares for the same money. The beauty of mutual funds is that you don't have to buy whole shares, you just decide how much money you want to invest, and the company will credit your account with a fraction of shares.

Not all mutual funds pay a dividend, but most do. Typically, mutual funds will reinvest dividends, so you are increasing your wealth as dividends automatically buy more shares in your account. This is not as exciting as watching hot stocks double in value overnight, but it is far less risky. There's nothing wrong with risk, as long as it's an educated risk, and you're risking what you can afford to lose.

There is an exception to buying individual stocks through a brokerage company. This is something banks and brokerages will not tell you about. Why? They don't make money from you. Sometimes you can buy stocks directly from the company. Blue-chip companies, such as Johnson & Johnson (JNJ), 3M (MMM), Hormel Foods (HRL) and many others have direct purchase plans at no fee. You can decide how much you want to invest regularly and the company sends you a statement, usually every three months.

DRIPs (Stock Reinvestment Plans) work in the same way as regularly investing in a mutual fund. But instead of a portfolio of stocks in a mutual fund, you're buying shares in just one company. These plans are not for day traders. They are definitely a buy-and-hold strategy. Here is the problem: There is no instant selling at the press of the keyboard key as you would with a brokerage account. When it comes time to sell, you'll have to make a phone call and fill out paperwork. Who knows what the price will be when you actually come to sell.

The stock market isn't for everyone. If you have credit card debt, it would be wise to pay that off first. Beware of the margin account. I'm not against buying individual stocks. I still have some from before the crash, but for most people buying a well-diversified mutual fund is a reasonable way to build wealth slowly. Remember Cramer's definition of mad money: that's the money you can afford to lose, but expect to win.

Soul-searching

When I lost my fortune in 2008, I couldn't sleep. My mood suffered. I couldn't tell anyone about it because I didn't want to be labeled a loser. For a year-and-a-half, I was in bad shape. My sense of self got a hammering. But I couldn't give up because people look to me to lead. I'm the rags to riches success story.

This painful stock-market event showed me that money is a means to an end, and not having it isn't the end of the world. But for all the euphoria of winning in the stock market, the emotional pain of losing is far, far worse.

I did a lot of soul-searching. I gave myself pep talks. I still had my veterinary business, and it was doing well. I was still getting money from my rental properties. I continued to invest in myself. I kept reading. In Robert Kiyosaki's book, *Rich Dad, Poor Dad*, he writes, "broke is temporary, poor is eternal", and "failure inspires winners, and defeats losers." When I discovered that many entrepreneurs had lost their fortune, only to make it back again, I thought to myself: *That's going to be me!*

The turning point came as I was driving around Warner Robins.

CHAPTER 8

Rebound

L ate 2008 was a tough time for me. I lost my fortune. How can you tell someone you've lost almost a million dollars? I couldn't. I kept it to myself. I had many sleepless nights. One night I woke up in a sweat. I got it! Almost every millionaire in every book I've read says that most millionaires had made it, lost it, and made it back again. I realized what I had to do.

Not long after my nighttime flash of insight, I was driving through an affluent neighborhood. I saw a huge house that didn't look like the others. It was a monstrosity, almost 10,000 square feet, but in a really nice neighborhood. Weeds grew in the yard. It was an unfinished eyesore.

I later learned it had been that way for three years. The neighbors wanted to push it down. I thought it had potential. I'd never rehabbed a house that big before. But I knew this house could be my big break.

I knew I could get cheap labor. Most construction workers were unemployed. Because nobody was buying, I negotiated deals with big box hardware stores.

I read somewhere that it's better to risk being thought a fool by keeping your mouth shut than to open it and remove all doubt. Trying to build a 10,000 square-foot house on a shoestring in the middle of a recession was foolish. And doubly foolish because I had no experience.

I didn't know what I was doing. But I knew this, nobody was gonna outwork, outthink, prepare and study harder than me. I always bet on myself. I figured I could read and feel my way through it until my mind caught up with my ambitions.

But one thing I knew was I needed to protect my ass from the inspectors, and make sure they were on board with my big plans. So I woke up one bright Monday morning and I went to talk to Mr. Mulkey, the director at the planning and zoning department. He was head of code enforcement for the city. I didn't know him at the time. But I knew he was the head honcho and had authority to shut down a project. I needed him to be on my side.

I told him I didn't know how to build a house, had never built one, but I had some rentals and was really good at rehabbing old houses to make them like new. I showed him the big monstrosity. I talked to him about my plans to make it the nicest house in the neighborhood. He knew of the house as he had received numerous complaints wanting it torn down. He told me he would help by giving me some pointers. That was good, but I needed more help than that.

When I was building my house I didn't know whether electrical or plumbing came first. I didn't know about permits.

Mr. Mulkey told me he'd help.

I shut up and listened to what he had to say. I may not understand everything someone is saying at first, but I shut up and listen. I can always read and find out. Again, better to be thought a fool than to open your mouth and remove all doubt.

So I had secured the contract for the house and got the building inspectors on board. Now for the hardest part of any project: getting the money to bring it to fruition. I had all these big plans to gain my fortune back, but I was down to my last investible $60,000. And in 2008, banks were in trouble. Foreclosures were mounting. Banks had a lot of properties on their books they wanted to get rid of them. They weren't interested in selling real estate loans. How in the world was I to take this measly $60,000 during a housing crisis and build a million-dollar home? But I did.

When you go to a bank and ask for a loan, the banker you talk to rarely decides. Instead, the loan officer goes to a committee and makes the case to loan you money. I tried it. I started off with Colony Bank. I had banked there for almost 10 years at the time, had multiple accounts and a banking history with them.

I showed the good people of Colony Bank the house, the plan, and everything to capture value. I like the people at Colony Bank, but not their policy. For me, the answer was no. They wouldn't give me a loan. This is why I tell people not to be loyal to a bank because whether you've been a client for five days or 50 years, they will only be loyal to their own business interest. That's just the banking process.

Being told no by Colony Bank was the first time I was told no since I started in business. And to this day, it's the last time I was told no. I still do business with Colony Bank. They're conveniently close to my veterinary practice. Brandy, the bank's office manager, takes great care of me and keeps me straight. We talk weekly, and there are no hard feelings.

In all the chaos of 2008, banks were running scared. They weren't interested in real estate projects, especially one where a veterinarian inexperienced in construction was trying to be a general contractor. But I wasn't about to take no for an answer. Somebody out there would bet on me.

Banks make money by loaning it out. I knew that if they wouldn't approve a loan, somebody else would.

Personal relationships matter. I circled around to my old friend Mac at Citizens Bank and Trust. I told him I thought I could make this eyesore into something wonderful. He said, "I know you can. I'll get you the money."

I learned this about negotiation: if they like you, they'll find a way. There's always a way, but you must beat down enough doors, speak into enough deaf ears, and convince others to bet the farm on you. Being "Dr. Hodges" has opened many doors for me; being "Vernard," a southern gentleman from humble beginnings, has kept them open. People do extra things for you only if they like you. So, treat others with respect and hope they reciprocate.

With Mac on board, I went to the bank and made an offer on the house. In my mind I was thinking, okay if I can get it for $250,000, it's a win. Yet, I used my poker face and relied on my first-person-to-throw-out-a-number-usually-loses mantra. I negotiated good terms and got the house for $160,000. The land by itself was worth $110,000.

When I signed the papers at the bank, I saw they had already loaned the foreclosed buyer $569,000. The bank took a hit, but they needed to raise cash. I spent another $250,000 to finish the house. I put in a pool and bought the lot behind me, where I built a 2800 square-foot four car garage with guest quarters.

My costs all in were $420,000. The appraisal value was over $900,000. My plan was to live in this house, refinance it, pull out my equity and use it to buy more rental properties. This time I would build wealth through real estate bricks and mortar instead of numbers on a computer screen, stocks.

Regaining confidence

I lost confidence in myself when I lost so much money in the stock market. Yet despite being mentally broken down, building my house helped me get back on my feet emotionally and financially. I learned about electricity, wiring, and plumbing. I learned about framing. I found out that you had to keep the walls open until the inspector signs off on electrical and plumbing. Only then could we put up insulation, sheetrock, painting, and flooring. I learned to be a general contractor.

And then I had to learn about the people side of the business. In the construction, business companies bid on projects. That means there are winners and losers. As a veterinarian in a caring profession, my nature is to be kind. Initially, I had a hard time telling people no, and that they did not win the bid. But I learned it's not personal, it's business. I have to look out for my best interests. Fortunately, most people in construction understand the bid process. Sometimes people come back and asked me why they didn't win the bid. This is not because they're mad at me. They want to learn how to do better.

The outside structure was solid. The roof was fine, but I had to gut everything else. I put in new wood floors and walls. Building my own house in this way gave me the confidence I could build anything I needed.

Now I got cocky. I was feeling like I could build anything. People were telling me, with a house like that you've got to have a pool. They didn't know I only had about $15,000 left to finish the house.

I didn't know a thing about swimming pools. I swim, but most black folks I know don't fool with pools, and nobody I knew had one. I didn't know what type of pool to get, vinyl lining, Gunite (a mixture of cement and sand) or fiberglass.

The swimming pool guy shows up and gives me an estimate of $75,000. The price was for the pool and some landscaping. I knew that wouldn't work. I researched swimming pools. I found a place outside of Atlanta that builds pools and helps homeowners install them. This sounded good.

I decided I'd build my own pool. How hard could that be? It's a hole in the ground. I hired people to dig a hole. I bought a fiberglass pool and it took two trucks to deliver it. I rented a huge crane. They picked up the pool from the trucks and lifted it over the roof of my house into the backyard. I had a friend come in, and we laid grass sod ourselves. The job was done for a third of the estimate. That was a big confidence builder.

The neighbors have gone from objecting to the eyesore, to telling me they should've bought that house. There's not a day goes by without people telling me how beautiful my house looks. A new house next door was recently purchased for $1.7 million.

Buying spree

By 2009, banks were afraid the federal government would come in and close them down. Banks had a lot of real estate loans that weren't being paid, and they were now desperate to get rid of bank-owned properties. I went on a buying spree. I figured people always need a place to live.

When foreclosed houses come up for auction they can only be purchased with cash. And I had cash from refinancing my new home.

I said to Stacy, my realtor, "Let's go get 'em."

"What does that mean?" she said.

"A monkey can buy a hundred dollars' worth of real estate for $100. I need to buy $100 for $60."

Warren Buffett became the richest person in the world in 2008. I read his books. He wrote that the right time to buy is when there's blood in the water. I look for price first. If it's low, I'll look at it. I look for trends. If all the other houses are $100,000 and this was $70,000, you know there's something wrong. And back then in 2009-2010, almost all houses were on sale.

I bought a house on Jerusalem Church Road in the best school district. It was $115,000 house in the "high-cotton" neighborhood. I said, "Offer them $60,000 cash." They took it.

I bought another house in the same neighborhood. I offered $50,000. They took it. I repeated this procedure often. I was constantly paying cash and getting houses for less than half of what they were worth. Each time I remodeled the house I could refinance and use that money to repeat the process. Today I own 100 doors, that's real estate talk for 100 units.

Branching out

One afternoon, I was in my office with Stacy. We were looking at two duplexes on a popular road. The realtor was someone I had heard Stacy talk to on the phone in the past.

"Damn! Don't you know this guy?" I said.

She said, "Yes, I do know him."

"Then why don't I own these?"

She said, "You're not interested in multifamily homes."

She was right. Investment gurus will tell you to buy multifamily houses, but that's not my system. I like single-family houses, although they cost more. I've had great success with them in the past, so why change? It's true that a multifamily house will only need one roof, or one heating system. However, people move in and out more frequently in a complex. Renters in a single-family home stay longer. But I wanted to look, and maybe make my first foray into multifamily 2property.

Stacy arranged for us to see the property. The duplexes were run down. I made an offer, and by the end of the day, I owned two duplexes. I inherited tenants; a group of cool Hispanic guys lived in one unit. They said they'd been there for five or six years and wanted to remain tenants. They still live there to this day. I renovated the other three units. Those turned out to be some of my best investments, and fueled my desire for more multifamily housing.

Not long afterward, I was talking to my mentor, Steve Rigby, who lives close by. He owns an amusement business and over 1000 rental units. He makes himself available to me to talk about real estate. I'm grateful to him for sharing his knowledge and wisdom. He said I needed to buy apartment buildings and get away from the single-family homes.

He explained how much of a cash cow the apartments could be, and the benefits of having everything under one roof. I'm always willing to listen to those who have gone to the places I'm trying to go. I learned about an 18-unit apartment complex coming up for sale that wasn't yet listed.

I went to see it. It was in a sad state. This turned out to be my other foray into multifamily housing.

I bought it for a quarter of the price it was worth. But it was emotionally draining. Scaling up has its headaches. You go from buying one toilet to buying 20. The building was in bad shape. It'd been neglected for a long time and there were vagrants living in it. The city had considered tearing it down. Again, I went to talk to my old friend Mr. Mulkey at the city planning department and told him my thoughts. He told me to go for it. I learned the city was making investments on that side of town.

I knew I could turn the all-brick apartment building around. I'd read that the city was putting in a park right next to the building. The good news was that it wasn't just talk, it happened. And that increased the property values. Today, there is a beautiful walking park with a lake and fountains right next to the apartment building I own.

The biggest part of turning a property around is to control access. So, the first thing I did was to build a fence around it. Then, I tore up all the rotten floors. I put in upscale flooring, upgraded amenities, stainless steel appliances, quality chandeliers. Because I bought it at such a good price, instead of going cheap, I made it a nice place to live. And it worked out. The place has stayed full from day one.

One afternoon, a lady called me looking for a place to house someone. It turned out that she was the liaison officer for the Veterans Association. She looked at the apartments and went back to talk to her colleagues who had other veterans who needed housing. Within a week I had seven new tenants, and the government was paying their rents. It didn't take me long to fill the rest of the vacancies. I had trouble coming up with the name of the apartment building. I got to thinking, with the new park next door and my apartments overlooking the lake, I'll call it Overlook Park. And that's the name it has today.

Flip

I went back to buying single-family houses. I'm not a house flipper. But I'm always looking for opportunities. It was about this time I bought a double-wide trailer. It was a nice trailer. I paid $13,000 for it. New air conditioning and some upgrades cost me another $4,000. Trailers break down over time so I knew I didn't want to hang onto it. I didn't want the headache of renting it, so I put it on Craigslist and here's what I wrote:

Why pay rent when you can own your own home? I'm passing on a blessing to you. $10,000 down, $55,000, and I'll be your banker.

Three days later I had a buyer. I financed it over nine years. He pays me $617 a month which covers the taxes and insurance. He will own it in about seven years and I'll probably make about $70,000 over the project. I'm not a house flipper, but when an opportunity presents itself, I'll do whatever deal makes sense. I'm willing to try new things.

Then a realtor called me about a huge house in one of the best school zones. It had a small two-bedroom house in the back. The whole thing was only $80,000. It would make a good rental so I bought it and spent $20,000 on upgrades.

Two weeks later, the realtor called me back and asked me if I would sell the house. She said she had a family ready to buy. I said it wasn't for sale, but if you made me a reasonable offer I'd consider it. She offered $175,000.

Three weeks later I had a contract on the house for that price. I almost doubled my money.

Better than flipping

While this deal made sense, I don't particularly like being a flipper. I actually like to buy and then beautify a home, with my little extra touches like tile showers, tile backsplashes, and attractive hardwood floors. Those details surprise people. It gives me joy to know I'm providing affordable and quality housing for people who wouldn't otherwise get it.

Another reason not to be a flipper is I don't want to pay the taxes on real estate sales. Short-term capital gains tax takes a big chunk out of your profit. You can do a 1031 exchange, but that's complicated. As long as you can put that money into another property, you avoid taxes, but it's a difficult process.

Renting out properties is all about cash flow, and that provides me a decent living. Depreciation is a big benefit to landlords. It's as if the government pays you to own the building. Here's how it works. Just about everything wears out. It doesn't matter whether it's your shoes, a car, or a house. The Internal Revenue Service (IRS), gives landlords a break. Each year you can deduct the estimated cost of wear-and-tear on rental property. It's called depreciation.

A residential building is assessed on the land and building value. Let's say the land value is $80,000 and the building value is $120,000. Land isn't going to wear out, so no tax break there. But the building will break down over time. The IRS figures that a residential unit has a useful life of 27.5 years. Don't ask why. It's the IRS. The good news is you get a tax break each year of the building's assessed value divided by its useful life. In this example, each year you can deduct approximately $4,364 ($120,000/27.5 years.) It's not what you make, but what you keep. Taxes play a big part of what you get to keep.

BRRRR

Just about anyone can use BRRRR, a five-part method to accumulate wealth through buying rental property. BRRRR stands for Buy, Rehab, Rent, Refinance, and Repeat.

When you use BRRRR, you own the asset. The renter pays your note. But what if you don't have enough for your first down payment or cash to remodel? One answer is syndication.

Other people's money

Syndication is where a group of investors pool their money to share risk and reward. This is called equity participation and is usually done in real estate through a Limited Liability Company (LLC) or Limited Partnership (LP). Syndication can be among individuals, for example, a bus driver, nurse, and a school teacher can form an LLC or an LP to buy real estate. As part of a real estate investing team, don't use all of your own money. If the LLC has three members and they all contribute the same amount, then each person would have an equal vote on decisions about which properties to buy, and operations, such as what fixtures you'll put into your building, or how much rent you will charge. So this is important to choose members wisely.

If you form a Limited Partnership (LP), then only one person, the managing partner, manages operations. This might be someone who contributes "sweat-equity" or special skill such as construction experience or management instead of cash. The managing partner of an LP gets to use the money and makes all the decisions. An LP needs at least one "general" (managing) partner and one "limited" (silent investor) partner. Limited investors are silent partners who contribute money, but have no say in the operations, and their losses (if any) are limited to what they put in.

But the managing partner is personally responsible for the business. If the money raised by the syndicate is for a down payment and the project goes bad, the managing partner is on the hook for paying back the whole loan and all business debts.

And here is something to watch out for. While there are exceptions in some states, if a silent partner of an LP starts to actively participate in the business, they become liable for anything that could go wrong just like the managing partner. So, if you don't play by the rules, you lose protection. Risk and reward go hand in hand.

Bird dog

Another way to earn money without using your own cash is to become a bird dog. A bird dog finds real estate opportunities. I was my own bird dog when I found the eyesore that turned into my beautiful home. I noticed the dilapidated state of the building and saw its potential. A bird dog is like a detective tracking down distressed properties. Does a house have a notice of foreclosure on the door? Does the property look in disrepair? Is it empty? A bird dog can read the signs. The bird dog passes leads to real estate investors. In return, the bird dog charges a fee.

Many real estate investors with no money got started this way. A bird-dog can use other techniques to make money in real estate with no money down. But it's mostly about being on the lookout for the right properties and selling those leads to real estate investors. You're getting paid for your time, knowledge, and effort. Eventually, you can use the money you make from bird-dogging to invest in your own properties.

You'll need to understand what real estate investing is about and how it works. You've already got some idea from reading this far. Next, make connections with real estate investors in your community. A bird dog is just one member of a real estate investing team. There are others.

My crew

You need a real estate team. Building it is the most important thing you can do. The beauty of it is most of your team members will provide you help and guidance free of charge. Here is what a typical team looks like: a real estate agent, a banker, or other hard money lenders, an insurance person, construction people, and an accountant to make sure you're not paying too much, or too few taxes. You are going to pay your accountant, but what you pay is likely to be a bargain, because otherwise, you would have to pay more in taxes. Your team members should be a phone call away, ready to dive in and help at a moment's notice. You need them to be there to help evaluate a potential deal at any time day or night.

I never stop learning. I've always looked for mentors; people who can help me learn what I need to know. When I was a kid, my mentors were my fraternity brothers. I learned a lot from them. I learned it pays to be nice. I learned to shut up and listen. If it hadn't been for my real estate mentor Rigby, I wouldn't be making over $10,000 a month from my Overlook Park complex.

Today, my real estate agent is Helen Hunt. We know each other well. When I want to buy a property she makes it happen—fast. She knows what I want and doesn't waste my time with irrelevant deals. She only brings me properties that fit my money-making criteria.

I've known my boy "Chicken" Lazarus Carter for almost 30 years. He specializes in manicuring yards, making them ready for new tenants. I'm fortunate to have him on my team because properties I buy are in disrepair and are in need of a little love. Typically, yards are unkempt with overgrown vines and bushes. With Chicken on my team, I keep the money in the family by paying a childhood friend to help keep properties looking good.

My first banking mentor was Mac Harden. He was a people's banker. He believed in me early on when I wanted to buy my own house. Before that, he made it possible for me to build my second Critter Fixer. Earlier when I didn't have cash, I would call Mac and tell him I wanted to buy a house. And he'd help out.

Unfortunately, Mac did that with unscrupulous people who borrowed money to build and never paid back the bank. I call them "Big Hat, No Cattle." These are guys who ride around in the big, jacked-up trucks and call themselves builders, but they never build anything. They buy some land and try to become builders. They borrow money but had no clue how to build. It was all talk and no action. They never delivered or paid off their loans. They were fraudsters.

When everything went belly up in 2008, the Big Hat, No Cattle guys just walked away from their loans and declared bankruptcy. This left my guy Mac out to dry. Mac was holding the bag with bad loans, so he got fired. I paid back every dime I borrowed.

Today, Clay is my main banker, and we've become good friends. Clay was a junior banker back in 2008. He inherited my friendship from Mac. I taught Clay as much as Clay taught me. The lesson here is, don't go to a banker when you need money. Form a relationship first. Clay and I would spend a long time together. He was a young guy with new responsibilities, but he realized that I was smart. He knew I had a system and was good for my outstanding loans.

Jessie is an old southern gentleman. He is always well groomed. I like him. He's a roofer by trade, but he does a lot more than that for me. He works on all my properties. I told him I don't want to have roof problems, four to six years later. I don't want to deal with them when they break. I want you to go to every property and tell me how much it would cost to put on new roofs.

He came back and said, "Doc, you got about two years left on nine of the roofs." I said, "Let's go to Lowe's [a building supply chain] and replace every one of them."

Jessie gave me a great price. Now I have 30 years on those roofs, and the job kept Jessie working. I learned about volume discounts at places like Lowe's. Buying in bulk is a big money saver, so replacing all the roofs at once was good for Jessie, good for the tenants, and good for me.

Another member of my real estate dream team is Andy Thomas, my insurance guy. With a simple phone call, I'm able to gather info about a house. He'll tell me how much my insurance and liabilities will be. If the home is in a flood zone, I'll know in a matter of minutes.

Richard Smallwood is my accountant and tax guy. He keeps me on the straight and narrow with the IRS. At the same time, he'll make sure that I enjoy the generous tax breaks the IRS offers for real estate owners. These people are my dream team. They take care of the details, and that frees me up to do what I love, looking for new opportunities.

Leadership is essentially about awareness and initiative; seeing an opportunity, assembling a team, and making it happen. After my stock-market losses, building my own house was good business, and it was also good for my emotional life. It gave me something to do where I could see the result. It threw up problems like building my swimming pool at a price I could afford. Solving the problems helped me rebuild my confidence. And that renewed confidence led me to expand my operation, connect with new people, and start new ventures.

CHAPTER 9

My first love

L ast night I got up in the small hours to do a C-section. I may not be able to hit a baseball out of the park or dunk a basketball, but I can deliver puppies in the middle of the night. And that gives me a great sense of accomplishment. I've always loved animals and I feel blessed that I became a veterinarian.

Although I'm an entrepreneur, veterinary medicine is my first love. I got into real estate because of the needs of my veterinary business. And that's been a great benefit as I explore opportunities to contribute to my community while making a good living. Several physician friends have told me they envy my lifestyle. I get to enjoy playing with puppies, but being a vet is more than playing with animals.

Veterinary medicine has become a fashionable career choice. In the popular imagination, veterinary medicine is arguably the most admired career, ranking right behind firefighters. Many kids I talk with want to become vets.

Their parents also think it's a good idea. It sounds like a wonderful job working with animals.

And they are right. Veterinary medicine is an incredible field. It's diverse, offering all kinds of medical specialties. Yet "vet med" is one of the most competitive professions to get into. According to the Association of American Veterinary Medical Colleges, there are only 30 accredited veterinary schools in the United States. And they take only 60 to 75 kids each year. A vet needs intellect, skill, and talent.

Rapid change

My time at Tuskegee College of Veterinary Medicine was tough. I struggled academically and financially. But I worked hard and made it through. When we were setting up Critter Fixer, we didn't have the toys we do now, like lasers and digital x-ray machines. We used that old x-ray machine from the 1940s. It took 45 minutes just to develop the picture. Today, that's all changed. I can now get a digital image in just five seconds.

Telemedicine has made great leaps forward. It's not just me anymore. I can be on the phone with a specialist at any university in the United States within five minutes. We can do EKGs, a test that checks for problems with the electrical activity of the heart. The cardiologist sees what I'm seeing, and we can discuss the results in just a few minutes. Rapid change is constant in this profession. Technology is always changing. If you're standing still in this profession, you're left behind. As new discoveries in medical science and patient care continue to improve, we must continually keep up with the times to stay on the cutting edge.

We do that through continuing education. We must renew our license every two years with the State of Georgia. I have to continually learn and adapt. I subscribe to many professional journals, and I'm constantly reading. I can't read everything in them regularly, but I read them often and they help me stay focused on what's happening in the veterinary field. As I connect with other specialist professionals, my knowledge base is ever expanding. And the clients also know more, too. More than ever people are researching their pet's condition on the Internet.

Good medicine is good business. Today, many medicines, say, for chemotherapy, are the same for humans and animals. I have a Drug Enforcement Administration (DEA) license, and that's something else to be continually renewed. This license allows me to call in pet medicines to a pharmacy. Veterinary medicine in many instances is on a par with human medicine.

A long road

Becoming a vet today is expensive. Typically it takes at least eight years of schooling. At the time of writing, starting salaries are approximately $70,000. The median is $88,000. The median meaning there were just as many veterinarians making less than $88,000 than making more. Competition for jobs is stiff.

School costs vary by which state you live in. According to the Association of American Veterinary Medical Colleges, the median annual tuition for out-of-state students is over $50,000 and about $24,000 for in-state tuition. For a huge investment of time and money, the financial reward is relatively low. You must have a plan. Think long-term. What is your return on your investment of time, energy, and money?

Eighty-eight thousand dollars might sound like a lot of money, but if you have a massive debt you could be underwater for many years. A report in the New England Journal of Medicine found that veterinarians had the highest debt-to-income ratio of all medical professions. Unless you bet on yourself by setting up a practice of your own, the investment in education and training may outweigh the benefits. The good news is there are other faster, more practical, and less expensive routes people can take to work with animals; for example, veterinary technicians, pet groomers, or animal trainers.

Becoming an insider

My partner, Terrence, and I have been taking emergency call for the last twenty years. We switch off with each other. One week, Terrence is on call. The following week it's my turn to get up in the middle of the night. Last night it was my turn delivering puppies. A seventy-five hour work week is brutal. Yet Terrence and I love our work so much we were prepared to keep taking emergencies until we died.

That changed when I got a phone call several months ago. The caller was Dr. Mike Younker, CEO of South Atlanta Veterinary Emergency and Specialty Center. He asked me to come to a meeting of veterinarians. He assumed I was connected with this veterinarian group and I knew what was going on. But I didn't. When Terrence and I got there, we learned about a plan to build a veterinarian emergency center for Middle Georgia. We were the only black guys in a room full of reputable veterinarians within a fifty-mile radius. At first, I felt a little intimidated. Some are third-generation veterinarians. Yet they wanted us to be part of it.

Respect from your peers is bigger than money. It made me feel good to be asked because not every veterinarian was asked. And this was proof that a poor black kid starting out picking peaches can earn the respect of the community. I went from being an outsider to an insider.

In the last chapter, I wrote about how syndication works. Now, I became a shareholder in Middle Georgia Veterinary Emergency Center, Inc. The project makes good sense. There isn't another emergency center within a seventy-five-mile radius, and it will serve pet owners as far away as 100 miles.

We are a group of veterinarians including a six-person board of directors. We've partnered with Crestview Animal Hospital LLC in Atlanta. That organization brings management experience and access to specialist care, such as cardiology, neurology, ophthalmology, and more. The Middle Georgia Veterinary Emergency Center is being staffed with emergency-trained veterinarians and technicians.

As I write this book in the summer of 2017, Middle Georgia Veterinary Emergency Center is about to be opened. For the first time in twenty years, I won't have to take emergency calls. No longer will I arrive in my driveway exhausted from a long day at work, only to get a call, turn around, and go back out again. I'm looking forward to more sleep. And that makes me happy.

Dogs don't pay bills

You can't just be good with a scalpel; you must be a business person, too. Unfortunately, all veterinarians don't have the business skills to make their practices financially successful. A successful vet is good with pet owners, and their pets.

Animals are a great comfort to people. Pets are members of the family. I love this job because it connects me to people and their pets.

Over the years, many pet owners have become like family. From my office, I've seen their lives play out. I've watched people have babies. I watch people go through cancer. I've been there for clients after their spouses have died. And I've cried with them. I've been the only black guy at bar mitzvahs and funerals. I've served as a pallbearer for a few clients when they have passed on.

I care for the police dogs at the Warner Robins Police Department. I've become friends with a number of dog handlers. I care for their safety. I want each one to have healthy canine partners.

Being a vet is an expression of love. People come in, they give me a hug, and we talk. And this has embedded me in my community. I never imagined it would be like this. A football coach asked me to speak to a group of kids. I speak at churches. Teachers ask me to speak to their students. Because I speak to groups, counties from outside have asked me to speak. But time is limited, and I must pick and choose. But I try to do as many as I can.

I have the experience, and I know what I'm doing. I know how to talk to clients. It used to take me 30 minutes to spay a dog. Now it takes nine minutes. Many times when I watch a dog walk into the exam room, I already know what's wrong.

It's amazing what dogs eat. I've removed fishing lures from dogs mouths, even removed swallowed thong underwear. Sometimes it's hard to figure out what's going on with a dog that can't speak to you. One case that comes to mind is a spayed dog having problems. The dog's owner was a woman in menopause. She was using estrogen cream on her legs. I discovered that the dog had been licking this cream, and that's what was causing the problem—not obvious.

Emotional intelligence

One day Gary Rothwell showed up in the clinic with his 20-year-old cat. In the wild, a cat's life expectancy is four to five years. Domestic cats live between 13 and 17 years. At the time, Steve was head of Georgia Bureau of Investigation (GBI) for Middle Georgia. Steve is tall, a nice guy, and he carried a gun.

I examined his cat, Kitty. Kitty was dehydrated and in bad shape. At 20 years old, this cat already had a long life. I diagnosed Kitty with kidney failure. Steve had tears in his eyes. He said, "Doc, I can go to a crime scene and see blood and guts, but this is tearing me up."

I was thinking *this man steps over dead bodies in the street all the time. Kitty means so much to him.* So, I did some extraordinary things; new drugs, dialysis, and a change of diet. It's my job to educate the client. I taught Steve about home care and we got partial kidney function. Kitty lived for another two years. Steve was greatly appreciative. The experience gave me a real sense of satisfaction. He has since retired from the GBI, and we have become good friends.

I wouldn't be in the business if I didn't love pets. Perhaps that's just me, but I concentrate only on the bad outcomes. For example, I may see 85 patients in a single day and 83 have great outcomes. On my drive home from work, I'll think about the two that didn't do well. Perhaps there's nothing anyone could have done for them. Veterinary medicine isn't magic. But I always think about the few, and as long as I do, I know I'll always be an advocate for pets.

I wouldn't be where I am today without my core Critter Fixer dream team. I'm grateful to Andrea, Paul, Richard, Sierra, Summer, and Tammy for all the hard work they put in. When it's a hot and humid July day, and there are thirty people in the waiting room, Tammy can make everyone feel comfortable, because she knows everyone by name.

Andrea, my lead tech, orchestrates the staff like a quarterback during multiple life-threatening events. She puts everyone in the right place to save lives. I can rely on my dream team. I have two technicians who've been working with me for over 20 years.

I can deal with a lot of things; broken bones, taking out eyes, or amputating limbs. But if a pet is full of maggots, I get a surgical technician to clean that up first. I just have a thing about maggots. I took a while to assemble the right people. They allow me to do so much more. When a dog comes in bleeding, the team bursts into action. They'll have that dog ready for anesthesia, and prepared for surgery. I take the glory, but I couldn't do it without them.

I got a call after hours. I thought the guy had been drinking. The caller said, "Doc, my dog got hit by an airplane!" Even though I imagined he might be drunk, I went anyway. It sounded unlikely but there is an airstrip not far from my office. When I arrived at the clinic, there was the dog with half its snout chopped off. Just as an airplane was coming into land the dog had jumped up and was hit by the propeller. I did surgery and the dog survived.

It's not emotionally easy to euthanize somebody's pet, but I know I'm relieving suffering. I make a deal with the pet owner. I say, "If I euthanize your dog, will you bring a new puppy back to me?" I want to see the circle of life complete. Ongoing care and client education is an important part of the job. I take great pride in educating my clients about their pets. But not all pet owners look after their pets as they should. Sometimes people just don't know how. I spent money and time to learn. What's obvious to some people isn't obvious to everyone.

But neglect is a problem. Some of my team ask why I don't get more in the clients face about what they should do. But if I make a pet owner feel bad, they won't come back, not necessarily to me, but to any vet. If a pet owner doesn't come to a licensed veterinarian, then that pet may suffer from some unqualified back-street operation. I want my clients to be knowledgeable and to understand how to care for their pets. It's ultimately about the pet's well-being.

Entrepreneurial vision

Vision is imagining a future reality. I've spent some time thinking about how real estate and veterinarian medicine can combine. Every business starts with an idea. I have an idea for a mobile clinic for rural outreach. I'm now working on a unique kind of pet care. Technology extends our capabilities, and with some creative thinking, I see how I can create something entirely new. I'm in the preliminary stages of creating an upscale pet hotel, Paws & Claws Pet Resort.

At the time of writing, I'm working on sketches. We are offering a concierge service. There will be video monitoring so pet owners can see their pets. Do you want to skype with your pet? No problem. If you want Foo Foo to be carried around all day, we'll do it. And customers can see us doing it.

While Critter Fixer is thriving maintaining pet health, Critter Fixer and Paws and Claws will be two distinctly different enterprises. The separation is important because I want veterinarians to refer business to Paws and Claws with the assurance that Critter Fixer won't steal their patients.

Entrepreneurial vision is seeing a need and filling it. My starting point was my first love. But no matter what line of business you're in, I encourage everyone to have more than one hustle. Multiple streams of income make sense, because these days, most people can't rely on holding on to one job. A side-hustle or two spreads your risk if you get laid off. If one of your streams of income dries up, you've got other ones to keep you going. Look around and think: what else can I do?

Colin Powell, an American statesman, and retired four-star general, wrote that success is the result of perfection, hard work, learning from failure, loyalty, and persistence. I agree. I've been fortunate to find what I love to do. But, for me, success isn't worth much without making a positive difference to others in my community. And that's what the next chapter is about.

CHAPTER 10

Giving back

August 2005, Puerto Rico: I took a few days off for a birthday beach vacation. On Tuesday, the weather turned bad. TV stations were reporting a powerful tropical depression to the north of the island. The weather was getting worse. I thought to myself: *So much for a few days of birthday beach time.*

The next day, the weather system strengthened even further. They were now calling it Tropical Storm Katrina. And it didn't stop there. By Thursday the tropical storm turned into a hurricane. That day, the eye of the hurricane passed over the National Hurricane Center, Florida. Winds reached 94 mph. For six long hours, Katrina wreaked its destruction over the Everglades in Florida. Then it lost some of its energy. It was downgraded as it moved toward the Gulf of Mexico.

By 5 pm the next day, Katrina shifted course from the Florida Panhandle. It was now heading for the Mississippi/Alabama coast. The governor of Louisiana declared a state of emergency. The Louisiana National Guard delivered truckloads of water and food to the Superdome, enough for three-day supply for 15,000 people.

On Saturday afternoon, Hurricane Katrina strengthened to a category three hurricane. That's when New Orleans Mayor, Ray Nagin, called for a voluntary evacuation and announced a state of emergency.

On Sunday it got even worse. Just after midnight, Hurricane Katrina reached category four intensity. Powerful winds gusted at 145 mph. Seven hours later, Katrina had reached category five, the highest on the Safia-Simpson Hurricane Wind Scale. The area was experiencing sustained winds at 175 mph and gusts up to 190 mph.

By Monday, failures of levees protecting low-lying New Orleans caused massive flooding. Eighteen hundred and thirty-six people died in the disaster. More than half were senior citizens. The TV footage was compelling: desperate people stood on their roofs as the water levels rose. Katrina was a massive disaster.

I had to help.

I went home and made phone calls to my friends at the TV station and newspaper. At the time my network wasn't as big as it is today. Yet I knew people who I thought might help. Within two hours I'd got two huge U-Haul vehicles donated. Terrence and my fraternity brothers supported my effort. Within 36 hours we'd filled both trailers with emergency supplies, and food. I sent pet food and veterinary medical supplies.

So many people asked me how they could help. They gave me tens of thousands of dollars' in cash and gift cards. The response from my community was overwhelming.

My fraternity brothers, Terrence, and I drove those supplies down to New Orleans. The big-box stores were destroyed. People were standing in long lines to access supplies as they came in. We were handing out hundred-dollar gift cards to them. We gave them food, diapers, sanitary products, and many things they needed. People cried when they saw what we were giving them.

Even today people still talk to me about that event.

I responded because my heart told me to. I didn't do it to help my business. I try to keep my charity work and my business separate. Nevertheless, there have been people who brought their pets to me because of what I did during Katrina. You get support by giving support.

The more my career has blossomed, the more I've been able to give back to the community.

My foundation

Our kids are a worthwhile investment because they are the future. When I go and talk to kids, it has an impact. I'm a role model. And male role models are lacking in many African-American communities. If my mentors hadn't taken an interest in me, I wouldn't be where I am today. There are only so many hours in the day, but if I can help, I will.

Communities are not standing still. They are getting better, or they're getting worse. I always try to help kids looking to improve their community, whether that's needing uniforms for school, cleats for the soccer team, or help with buying a bus. I started by helping individuals in need. I'd pay people's electric bill, or buy them groceries. I bought gifts and food at Christmas for five kids in need, and then ten families. By 2011, my effort became Dr. Vernard Hodges, It Takes a Village Charity Foundation. It is a 501(c)(3) Nonprofit. It mainly teaches young people about business, but it also helps by providing necessities for people in need.

Last year, I teamed up with Kohl's, a department store retail chain. We sent thirty families on a shopping spree for Christmas.

I remember well a gentleman shopping with his little girl. His shoes were split in two and held together with duct tape. He apologized for getting there late. He told me how he had to take four bus transfers to get to the store. I pulled him aside, and said: "You get some shoes and what you need for yourself." He was grateful. The problem with Christmas for many people is it's just a swipe of the credit card. But this gentleman was making a huge sacrifice to give his children some pleasure.

As an ancient proverb says, "Give a man a fish, and you feed him for a day. Teach a man to fish, and you feed him for a lifetime." My charity helps kids to help themselves economically.

Connections

If you want to start a business, what can you do? I read, shut up, and listened. I found mentors. My degree opened doors. It didn't mean I was smart, but it gave me status, so I could connect with other professionals. But where in the African-American community can you go for help? There are two valuable networks, first, the Church, and second, the barbershop/beauty salon. These are community places where people connect face-to-face.

Everybody wants something

When I joined the Fellowship Bible Baptist Church I became good friends with the late pastor, Reverend Willie Reid. One day we were eating at the same restaurant. He said, "Hodges, come over here, I want to talk to you." He was a businessman. He owned a car lot, real estate, and he had his hand in several ventures.

Reverend Reid and I talked about the stresses of constantly being pulled in multiple directions. His phone rang constantly while we were eating. He said. "Just about every time my phone rings, it's always someone wanting something. I'm willing to give a handout, but it's better to give a hand up. Be thankful God had put you where you are, because, *to whom much is given much is expected*. Never take lightly being a pillar of the community, because someone is always watching." He was right, there are many people watching, especially my son.

Reverend Reid and I traded phone numbers. When I called he would say, "What do you want, Hodges?" I would reply, "I just called to talk, I don't want anything." We would laugh. It was our little inside joke because when either of us got a phone call it was usually somebody wanting something.

Success is a gift and a curse. It has its flaws. I help many people, but I have to say no sometimes. And when I do that, they think I'm mean, or I couldn't care less. But I do care. I've helped so many people with school. I help many people pay their bills. I've even paid for funerals. When you're a success everybody wants something from you. But you must know when to say no.

When you achieve a certain level of success in your community, people look up to you. They're watching your every move. And with that comes the responsibility to learn how to be a leader and do the right thing. If people are looking for you to lead, you'd better lead.

Reverend Reid and the Church helped nurture me. And I give back through tithing. When Reverend Reid passed away, Pastor Morgan took his place. He's also a nurturer of souls and has an entrepreneurial spirit. He owns a clothing boutique with his wife in Warner Robins.

Pastor Morgan has a strong desire to make sure the members of his flock become financially literate. The Church is a place where people congregate to seek knowledge. For three consecutive weeks during Bible study, he brought in Steve Williams, an early banking mentor of mine, to talk about finances, savings, investing, and business. If the Church is the first place where a community comes together, the second place (for men) is the barbershop.

Business at the barbershop

When you look good, you feel good about yourself. Barbering is a multimillion-dollar business. My barber, Luke, has been cutting hair for 35 years. He's been my barber for the last 20 years. When men wait at the barbershop, they talk. Sometimes people go to the barber at the same time each week and conversations can span weeks. This is where you can learn about what's going on in the neighborhoods.

I remember seeing a kid standing in one of Luke's chairs. Luke's reaction was to yell a few choice words, almost bringing the little boy to tears. Luke and I talked about the incident afterward. I told him he has status in the community as a business owner. And he should act professionally. Sure, a kid standing on a chair isn't acceptable behavior. But it's not professional to yell at a client. Are they likely to come back? No. Unfortunately, several barbers haven't learned to talk to their clients professionally. It's not about just cutting hair. It's about connection and customer experience.

"Man, you're right," said Luke when I went to see him the following week. Ever since Luke and I bounce ideas around. He's since moved into a bigger barbershop. He's an entrepreneur with six barbers working for him. He knows the business side. He makes sure his barbers are licensed and dress a certain way. They've learned to make their customers feel comfortable so they want to come back.

Luke is a very smart guy. Who can he talk to about making his business better? We talk about the barbershop environment. Where's the TV going to be? What sort of music is appropriate for his customers? When you're in your car you can listen to any music you like, but in a business, think of your customers. Some kids go to the barbershop with their mothers. You want to capitalize on every dollar. You don't want mothers saying I'm not going back to that barber. Think about what's fitting for customers. We are in a military town so professionalism matters. Small things have big effects.

I learn from Luke as well. He has his ear to the ground. Just like the lookouts in the Trap or the drug reps letting me know what's happening with other veterinary practices, Luke keeps me informed about what's going on in the neighborhoods.

Luke and I are friends. Yet we live in different worlds. On Monday to Friday, before work, I look at what stocks I'll buy or sell. I keep up with the financial news on CNBC. I get a call from the office to find out how my patients are doing. I go to the office, perform surgery, speak to clients, maybe meet with a banker at lunchtime, go back to work, deal with clients, checkup on tenants, and monitor my stocks. That's my day. But going to the barbershop keeps me grounded. I keep up with the latest lingo or fashions there. I learn what's going on in the daily lives of men who look like me, act like me, and come from the same places.

Loyalty

My friends and I grew up with the code "snitching ain't cool." It all comes down to loyalty. My childhood friend Marvin is serving a 10-year sentence for theft. We talk once or twice a week and I make sure he has enough funds to buy what he needs. We talk about how things could have been different. In Chapter 1, I told the story of him giving me $293,000 in cash to hold. If he had made different choices with that money he would be in a very different place today.

Why do I continue to bother with Marvin? I don't agree with some things he's done, but I continue to support him because if not me, then who? I can help someone to help themselves, but if they continue to violate that trust, then loyalty has its limits. After all, we are all grown men.

When we were young, none of us had enough knowledge to know what to do with money. It's a sad fate for Marvin who was a popular athlete and an otherwise smart guy. No one was leading to show him the way. When there are few options, people will do what they have to do to survive. That's just the way life is. Everyone has to eat.

The choice

Who contributes most to their community, a prisoner, or someone who's been to school and learned a trade? In

Georgia, the government spends more than twice as much on an inmate than it does to educate a student. According to the same U.S. Census survey, in some states that number rises to over five times as much. Without a legitimate way to earn a living for young people, our tax dollars will go to locking them up. Then, the whole community suffers. Isn't it better to invest in people so they don't have to resort to crime? It's better for them to become productive members of the community.

One way or another we'll spend our tax dollars. Here's a problem, Historically Black Colleges and Universities are under a lot of pressure. There are not enough funds. But if HBCUs are underfunded, many people—people like me—will fall through the cracks. And that's going to have a bad effect on the community for years to come.

Marvin was my best friend when I was young. Henry Howard was another close childhood friend. Henry and I graduated high school together. Like many of us in the Trap, he made some poor decisions. But then he went into the Marines. Later, he worked for the local utility department. Henry grew up in public housing in Fort Valley. He knew the hardships of growing up poor in the housing projects and wanted to give back to the hood. He and a group of his peers started a self-help group in Fort Valley.

Henry's group, Unity in the Community, helps people living in Fort Valley's housing projects. His group organizes health fairs, brings in speakers for educational events. The objective is to help people use resources to get better jobs and find a way out of the projects. I'm proud to say that Dr.

Vernard Hodges, It Takes a Village Charity Foundation, has teamed up with them on various projects

When no one is looking

Being a man is doing the right thing when no one is looking. Many of my personal values were shaped by my family, fraternity, the Church, and other people I've been fortunate enough to meet. I helped people when I heard they didn't have enough to eat. But no one else knew about it. Distressed mothers have called me about their kids failing in school, and I've reached out to their kids. Without male role models, young men are rudderless. I've had kids come to my home for a day or two so I could talk to them. Being a man is taking responsibility for what you do. It's being a martyr for a cause.

In 2015, when I heard about the shooting death of Jai'mel Anderson, an 8-year-old, it broke my heart. It happened in the Indian Oaks apartment complex, Fort Valley, which is next door to what used to be the Trap. Jai'mel was watching TV at the apartment of his mother's boyfriend when someone shot through the front door and killed him. Five men were charged with murder. But that wasn't going to bring Jai'mel back. I was so angry. This sort of thing just didn't happen when I was growing up. Guns were a rarity back then. People used to fight, but the next day they'd patch up their differences. The community was falling apart, and I had to give people in Fort Valley hope for a better future.

With the help of my classmate and friend Henry Howard, I held the "Rally in the Valley." Over 500 people came together to mourn Jai'mel's death. We talked about how our community can stop the violence. We provided free barbecue chicken and soft drinks. We had speakers come. It was so sad that it took this terrible event for people to come together to make a difference. But community support shows that people care. There is hope for our children. And hope for better is the first step in making our communities safer.

Gratitude

For many people, their pets are their only family. Multiple times I've been offered to be a beneficiary in pet owners wills because my care of their pets and the relationship with them has meant so much. I've known some since the beginning of Critter Fixer when I was struggling. They ask me if the business is okay, can I afford to eat, or can I afford to keep the lights on. It's funny how they still view me as fresh out of school, a much younger and poorer person than I am today. But I love it because they're my extended family who wants me to succeed.

When I was younger, I never knew the pleasures of giving back, because I didn't have much. My favorite Rapper Jay-Z said it well:

And I can't help the poor if I'm one of them

So I got rich and gave back to me

That's the win, win.

—*Moment of Clarity* [The Black Album, 2003]

Recently, my mother fell and broke her hip. After she got out of the hospital, she went to a rehab facility called the Lodge. The facility is very nice but after staying for over two months she was ready to leave. If you aren't walking, and aren't able to care for yourself, the next place you usually go to is a nursing home. My mother was worried about what the future held for her. I didn't tell her what I was doing. I wanted it to be a surprise. I was finalizing the interior of a new condominium I had bought for her. I was asking her about her favorite colors, what kind of furniture and lighting she would like if money was no object. But I didn't let on why I was asking these questions.

I'd found the property about five doors down from her good friend and my God mom Ms. Petties, and five minutes away from my house. I bought it at a great price and rehabbed it. I replaced all the doors with larger ones; made everything wheelchair accessible, furnished it in her favorite colors, and bought her a hospital bed. I planted her favorite rosebushes, and put a canopy on the back porch, so she could sit out and drink her coffee, even when it was raining. When her nurse wheeled her in for the first time I said, "This is your place. You can spend the rest of your life here, and you have your own nurse. You won't have to go to any place you don't want to." She burst into tears.

I feel blessed to be able to spoil my mom. My dad was generous and spoiled me with what he had, even if he had little. But the lessons he taught me about life have been invaluable. I feel blessed to spoil my son, VJ, and pass along the life lessons that my dad taught me. I must admit, my son is a terrific kid, much smarter than I ever was. He hasn't made a grade below A.

I love my son with all my heart. He is the reason I get up and work hard each day, so he will have a head start with tools to be much more successful than me. He recently took the SAT for the Duke Talent Identification Program (Duke TIP) scoring in the top 5 percentile of 7th graders in the country. With his high score, he has plans to follow in his dad's footsteps and become a veterinarian.

I'm successful enough to have the resources to choose what I want to do. I can go where I want, and dress any way I choose. I can travel. I can buy material goods. But one more car, or a bigger house, won't make me any happier. I've matured over the years.

What's meaningful for me is having the resources to help other people live a better life. And to live a better life you must understand personal finance; what money is and how it works.

CHAPTER 11

Money 101

I'm constantly asked about money and how to grow it. Financial literacy isn't taught in school. People want to learn about money management skills. But what gets taught in school is often decided at a national level. Without an understanding of money basics, young people in our communities will continue to make poor decisions with life-long consequences.

I'm not talking about complicated accounting, but simple ideas anyone can grasp. And it gets no simpler than this: if you spend more than you earn, you will be in trouble. If you spend less than you earn, you have a surplus. With that surplus, you can invest it so your money makes money all by itself.

Sound good?

There's an old saying that a fool and his money are soon parted. Sadly, this happens a lot. Too many people who've won the lottery have ended up bankrupt within just a few years. And this comes from lacking a basic understanding of money.

Needs and wants

Without money, you're in bad shape. If personal finance was taught in high school we would all be a lot better off. You need money to put food on the table. You need shelter and safety. You must look after your family. Those are basic needs.

Then, there are the wants. Maybe you want to look cool in new Nikes or be a girl magnet driving around in that immaculate car. Maybe you want to live in a big house, travel to exotic places, or help others. My advice is to take care of your basic needs first: needs before wants.

Let's look at needs. Psychologist Abraham Maslow created a five-part model of human needs, shown as a pyramid.

1. At the bottom of the pyramid are our basic needs: food, water, warmth, and rest. Without those we die.

2. Resting on the base is the next level: safety and security.

3. Once we are safe we can focus on "belongingness," being part of a group. This is where we develop friendships and intimate relationships.

4. This level is devoted to "esteem needs," accomplishment and prestige. Confidence comes through achievement.

5. At the tip of the pyramid is self-fulfillment needs. This is what Maslow calls self-actualization, achieving your full potential as a creative human. You make choices in life based on self-knowledge and an understanding of your own uniqueness.

Attitude

What is your belief about money? Could it be your attitude is holding you back? Your relationship to money depends on your needs, and your attitude. Perhaps you've heard that money is the root of all evil. The actual quote from the Bible is "For the love of money is the root of all evil..." Money itself isn't evil. It's a tool.

For some people, money is keeping score. Money can give you prestige. Another belief is that money will make you happy, and more money will make you even happier. But studies have shown that once you reach a certain level of wealth, more does little for you. Money allows you to find better opportunities, and eventually the freedom to do what you want to do.

Thornton Wilder, a writer, said it well when he wrote that money is like manure; it's not worth a thing unless it's spread around encouraging young things to grow.

Your situation

Businesses operate with a profit and loss statement (P&L). It's a snapshot of the business's financial health. You can do something like this on a personal level. Look at your net worth. Earlier, I explained net worth is simply your assets minus your liabilities, what you have, minus what you owe. All you need for basic personal finance it the ability to add and subtract.

Add up all of your bills, your rent or house payments, and what you spend on entertainment, food, and clothing. Now, subtract that from what you earn each month. The result will tell you whether you're saving for a better future or digging yourself deeper into a hole of debt.

If you owe more than you make, then you're a debtor. Earlier, I talked about good debt and bad debt. A mortgage is a good debt because you're building your wealth. Your house will probably increase in value. School debt is probably good debt — as long as you can make a living at what you're studying. Going into debt to fund a vacation, a luxury car or something that can't be sold later at a profit is bad debt.

Barack Obama said, "Money is not the only answer, but it makes a difference." Your goal is to build wealth for a better future. If you'll bet on yourself, you need something to bet with. And to do that, save money, and then invest it so your money makes even more money. But who has extra money? Very few people do. What if you're in deep debt and you can't pay your bills?

You'll need to separate your wants from your needs. The harsh reality is you have two options: you can earn more, or live on less. That's it. But before you can save, pay off your debts first. Here's why.

Credit danger

Personal debt has interest payments and other fees. A loan is made up of the principle, the amount you borrowed, and interest. Interest is the fee charged by the lender for lending you money. Starting out, you're high risk because you have no repayment history. You'll pay a high-interest rate. If you have good credit, you'll pay less. If you don't pay off what you borrow, you can end up in a bad way. Without a basic understanding of money, you can lose everything.

Beware of check cashing outfits. Payday loans carry extreme annual interest rates. How about 400 percent! Compare that with the average interest rate for a new credit card, 15 percent. Payday loans usually offer loans to cover an emergency of just two weeks. States are cracking down on them. They are generally illegal in Georgia, but there are exceptions. Avoid them if you can.

Once you're eighteen, you can legally get a credit card—if the bank will give you one. But banks aren't falling over themselves to give young people credit cards. Why? The reason is no credit history. Without a card, there is no record of you borrowing and paying back on time. And here is the paradox; you must have a credit card so you can pay it back, and you can't pay it back without a credit card. You need a credit history. So what can you do?

The way I did it was to get a prepaid reloadable debit card. You can get them from various retailers such as Walmart or CVS Pharmacy. They may require an activation fee, but they look like credit cards and are offered by Visa and MasterCard.

Alternatively, you can tie a debit card to your bank account. If you go this route, first open a checking account at a bank or credit union. I like small community banks. You'll need your social security number, ID, a mailing address, email address, information about your job, and some money to deposit. You'll fill out an application.

Ask the bank for a debit card tied to your account. If you have $100 in your account, you should be able to use your debit card up to that amount. You are establishing a financial history by using a debit card and making deposits to your bank account. Banks like that. With a history, you can now apply for a credit card. But be careful.

Many young people get into trouble with credit cards because they are not ready. You must keep track of your spending. There are online calculators to help you do this. For every dollar you spend, you must pay it back on time, or suffer extra fees. Details are often buried in the small print. Pay on time and consistently without someone there to remind you. Not paying attention is expensive.

Credit card companies make money by charging you fees and interest. You can avoid those fees if you pay off the entire balance each month. You may not be in a position to do that immediately, but make paying off the balance each month a goal. Once you get your first credit card, other companies will offer you credit cards. It may be tempting to accept them but stick with one credit card, at least for a while.

When you only pay the minimum each month it's good for the credit card company, and bad for you, really bad. If you have bad credit you may have to pay as much as 23 percent interest. Here's why interest can get you into trouble. I'm basing this on a common interest rate of 15 percent. A minimum payment of $10 a month on a balance of $1000 will never be paid off. Never is a long time. If you pay $20 a month, it will take eleven long years. Increase that to $100 a month and you'll pay it off in eleven months. You can use a credit card—or the credit card can use you. Knowledge is power.

Start from where you are

Pay off loans with the highest interest rate first. Your highest interest rate will probably be on a credit card. Make this a priority and do it as quickly as you can. Watch out! If you miss payments, then you must pay penalties and late fees. And that hurts your credit score. When it's time to buy a house you'll discover you have a bad credit score. And that could take a long time to repair. But even worse, your overall debt will balloon if you don't pay down your debts.

First, you should pay down as much as you can each month. But that's easier said than done. Where's the money coming from?

Ask yourself a few questions. What are your spending habits? This is something you must know. If you smoke a pack of cigarettes a day, you're spending about $2000 a year. One cup of coffee a day at Starbucks will cost you somewhere around $800 a year, and maybe much more if you're buying expensive drinks.

Small regular purchases add up. Keep track of them. What do you spend money on regularly? Can you cut some minor expenses through a change of habit? Could you take your lunch to work, and save on buying it out? Can you get a cheaper phone plan? How about that cable bill? Monthly charges are the killer. Time is the enemy when you're in debt.

The longer you're in debt, the worse it gets. But time is your friend when you're saving and investing regularly. It's the little things that seem like nothing, but a dollar here and a dollar there adds up. Don't think of money as what you can buy. Think of it as what you can do. This is how you bet on yourself.

Small savings, big results

Money habits are either good or bad. Saving a little money regularly is the path to wealth. Over time your cash can earn cash all by itself because you've gone from being a debtor to being a creditor. Instead of your debt digging you deeper and deeper into a hole, your wealth will increase. You'll be receiving interest and dividend payments.

Banks pay little on a savings account but start there. Put money in a savings account at a bank or credit union until you have saved up enough to invest it. Everyone has to start somewhere. This is not money for spending. You're going to invest it in yourself, or stocks, or bonds, or real estate; or some mixture of these.

Always save something

Ideally, you can save ten cents for every dollar that passes through your hands. If that's too much, make a habit of always saving something. Form a money habit. Seeing your money grow keeps you focused. Saving before spending is what's called paying yourself first.

You may set up automatic savings from your checking account with your bank. You could just stuff cash into a box at home, but there is the temptation to use it, or even lose it. No matter how you do it, try to always put away some portion of what you get. Being an ASS (Always Save Something) is cool.

Banks

A retail bank, the sort you see on Main Street, makes money by taking in deposits from savers and lending it to borrowers. As a saver, they give you maybe one percent on your money and lend it out at four percent, say, to someone who wants to buy a house, or a small business wanting to buy equipment. That's retail banking in a nutshell. They have related services and fees. Most banks charge you for maintaining your checking account. But not all do. Ask about free checking accounts. You must ask.

Many young people have never written a check because so many transactions are done electronically online. But if you're planning to be in business, learn what a check is and how to write one. A check is another means of transferring money between people and institutions. It works like a debit card because you're using money in your account without having to go to the bank, draw out cash, and use that to buy goods and services.

When you use your debit card at a store the merchant debits your bank account in the amount of the purchase. When you write a paper check, you fill out the name of the person or business you are paying, the amount of the purchase, and sign it. The check itself has your account number on it. Beware of accepting personal checks. They are easy to write, but if there is no money in the account of the payer, you are out of luck.

Another form of check is a cashier's check or bank check. This is a check written by the bank, using the bank's funds, and is much more secure.

If you write checks for more than is in your checking account, the bank will either deny the charge or slap you with overdraft fees. You can monitor your account online or the bank will send your monthly statement through snail mail.

Look for a free checking and savings account at a local community bank or a credit union. Credit unions offer checking and savings accounts, and they are not-for-profit. They can be a good deal because their earnings are paid back to its "members" in better savings rates and lower loan rates. Banks have customers, not members, and bank profits go to shareholders.

From saver to investor

According to a 2015-16 African American Financial Experience study of 1,043 African Americans, 52 percent said they were well prepared to make smart money decisions. But most were savers and not investors. Saving is a place to keep your rainy-day funds. If you're saving for a property down payment, a savings account is a good place. If you will need that money in three to five years, a savings account is a good place to stash your cash.

Each person has different needs. If you have a secure job, you may need less in your emergency savings account than someone starting a business. Remember to be patient when building wealth.

Save first, and then invest. By investing I mean putting money to work for you long-term, in stocks, bonds, or real estate. Investments can lose money and make money. If you have no emergency fund you may be tempted to sell when the market is losing money. That's something you want to avoid.

The Vanguard Group is a mutual fund company with some of the lowest fees. You can start by buying a mutual fund and making regular contributions to it. You can set this up automatically from your bank account.

Stocks and bonds go up and down over time, but the long-term trend is for stocks to increase in value. Bonds are IOUs; they don't go up and down so much as stocks do. But bonds pay you interest. Some stocks pay a dividend. Both are payments to you. Vanguard will automatically reinvest those payments in your mutual fund so it grows. This is the reverse of being in credit card debt.

The value of having a mixture of stocks and bonds is that typically when one goes up, the other goes down.

A good first investment mutual fund is the Vanguard Balanced Index Fund (VBINX). You'll need at least $3,000 to buy "Investor" shares. VBINX is an index fund which tracks the entire U.S stock and bond market in one fund, 60 percent stocks, and 40 percent bonds. The Balanced Index Fund will not make you rich overnight. But it has almost doubled in the last 10 years, just by reinvesting its interest and dividends. If you had contributed regularly you'd be even further ahead. Because this happened in the past, doesn't mean it will do that in the future. No one knows what the future will bring.

With the Vanguard Balanced Index Fund, you can make additional contributions in any amount over $1. You can set up regular payments from your bank account into your Vanguard account in small increments. Once you reach $10,000 you can convert to "Admiral" shares of this same fund and pay a lower expense fee.

When you don't have much money, you pay more in fees. When you have more money, you pay less. Over a ten year period and for every $10,000 invested you'd pay $337 in expenses for investor shares, compared to $1,449 for the category average. You'd only pay $125 for admiral shares. That's encouragement to invest long-term and build wealth. However, fees change all the time, and the overall trend is for them to go down and not up. You can find more information at https://personal.vanguard.com. Read the prospectus before investing.

The Vanguard Balanced Index Fund is a boring fund. And that can be a good thing. Maybe it's all you need as a good fund for a core holding. If you want to buy individual stocks or exchange-traded funds (ETF), you must open a brokerage account. But I suggest you can do that later—much later.

There is a lot to learn about investing, but this is a simple method to get you started.

1. Assess your money situation
2. Pay down your debt first
3. Be an ASS: Always Save Something
4. Save enough for an emergency fund
5. Use additional savings to invest in a balanced index fund with low fees
6. Watch your wealth grow

There are other life skills they don't teach you in school, and that's what I'll tell you about next.

CHAPTER 12

Life lessons

Even though I was poor growing up in a trailer park, I had the support of my dad. I could see how he would try just about anything to make a living. I was influenced by his love for animals. He had a kind heart. He raised cattle but didn't want to sell the calves. He was not a businessman, but he was enterprising. His interest in koi taught him to become an expert on ornamental fish. I was paying attention. I watched. I listened. I learned. Even though I didn't know it at the time, those early experiences set me on the path to becoming a veterinarian and an entrepreneur.

One of the most difficult questions in life is what to do with it. Who should you be? Should you be an athlete? Should you be a rapper? Maybe you can become an athlete or rapper if you have unusual grit and talent. The truth is somebody has to do it. But competition is stiff. The reality is most young black men will not have these glamorous occupations. So what do you do?

Here is the big question: Do you want to work for someone else, or do you want to work for yourself? My dad wasn't an employee. He tried different things to make a living. Even though he wasn't financially successful he was his own man.

Making a living

I started by being somebody else's employee before I went out on my own. I learned from my surroundings. Except for HBCUs, most school systems aren't set up for African-Americans to prosper. At the very least, school should set you up for making a living. But it doesn't. Mostly it sets you up for consuming more schooling. There's only so much preparing to prepare that students can take.

Going to technical school trains you for a specific job. And it's a good idea to know there is demand for the job you're training for. There are plenty of people with a lot of education—and school debt —without a way to make a living.

I'm a firm believer in technical education. I served on the State Board of the Technical College System of Georgia (TCSG) with campuses in Macon and Warner Robins. Under the leadership of Dr. Ivan Allen, these schools provide unbelievable economic impact. I've witnessed many successes. Students get first-class training in relevant skills to go into the workforce.

I talked earlier about the long and expensive training period for becoming a veterinarian today, yet some of the fastest growing occupations are veterinary technicians and technologists. The training takes only two years for a technician, and four years for a technologist. Then there's the Veterinary Technician National Examination (VTNE) to get your license. Veterinary assistants and office managers can start work after completing a short certificate program. And there are other animal-related jobs. With approximately 77.5 million dogs in the U.S., demand is increasing for dog trainers.

We all think that our community is our world. But the world is much bigger than your community. There are more opportunities than you can imagine. The government puts out reports on which jobs are projected to be most in demand. You can check out the Bureau of Labor Statistics (BLS) *Occupational Outlook Handbook* online at www.bls.gov. As of 2017, here are just a few of the many jobs you can start with a high school diploma or equivalent, or by going to a trade school.

Electrician

The median pay for electricians is $52,750 a year. You'll need a high school diploma or equivalent to start as an apprentice (on-the-job training.) Electricians are in demand and the job outlook is much faster than average over the next 10 years. This job isn't going to disappear overseas.

Plumber

The median pay for a plumber is $51,450 a year. This is another fast-growing occupation. Typically, plumbers start off as an apprentice to a master plumber. You need a high school diploma or equivalent. Like electricians, plumbers work in many environments; homes, construction sites, factories, and businesses.

HVACR technician

Heating, Ventilation, Air Conditioning, and Refrigeration (HVACR) technicians are in demand. Median pay is $49,910 a year after the technician has completed long-term on-the-job training.

Occupational Outlook Handbook is a valuable resource for jobs you would never think of. Under fastest growing occupations, the top slot is wind turbine service technicians; median wage $52,260 a year. Home health aides, commercial drivers, ambulance drivers, forensic science technicians, phlebotomists (people who draw blood), emergency medical technicians, paramedics, and solar voltaic installers are just a few of the projected fastest growing occupations over the next 10 years. A skilled job is a great foundation to branch out into self-employment or other entrepreneurial ventures.

Becoming "the man"

Self-employment isn't for everyone. To win, you will have to lose sometimes. About half of all new businesses fail within five years. Most don't have enough money to see them through the lean times. That's why you must get a basic financial education. But if you have the desire to learn, and the ability to stick with it when things are tough, being your own boss can be satisfying and rewarding. Schools don't teach you what you need to be self-employed, which is why you should read everything you can, and ask questions. Taking responsibility for your own learning is essential. With determination, you can move from employee to being your own boss.

So, how can you start? Get yourself in the right place. Respect, enthusiasm, and interest will take you a long way. In two words: be nice. If that's you, get your foot in the door. The foot-in-the-door technique is a way to persuade someone by making a small request now, and a larger one later.

Being an employee before starting your own business has many advantages. Most jobs aren't advertised. That's because employers would rather find someone they know, or someone recommended for a job—before advertising. And that's a good reason for getting to know potential employers.

Many organizations will let you volunteer. You get to see what's going on and get to know people. You discover if it's the work you want to do—or not. Knowing what's a bad fit for you is also valuable knowledge. You don't have time to waste. Often, the only way you can tell whether something will work is by doing it.

Volunteering is a learning opportunity, and you get the satisfaction of contributing to an organization. In business "contribution of value" is what everyone is looking for. That's why when you spend your money, you expect value in return. When you volunteer, you're likely to connect with people who can hire you, give you advice, or even become a mentor.

My mentors have helped me get to where I am today. A mentor is someone who can help you with your long-term development. Maybe you can find a mentor through your religious or volunteer organization, or your workplace. Mentors offer guidance, not how-to advice on specific skill development. That's the role of a coach. Mentors are there to support and encourage you on your chosen path.

Does where you volunteer match what you want to learn? If you want to be in law enforcement, it makes little sense to volunteer in a hardware store. The police department would be a better bet. Years ago when I didn't know about banking I would go to the bank, be quiet and observe. Shut up and listen is a valuable behavior. It doesn't cost a dime to go to the mall and watch a manager.

I have young people come in and shadow me in my veterinary practice. They can see what I do and how I go about my daily routine. Reliability is highly valued at work. Some people say they will come, but never show up. Others do what they say they will do. Those are willing to volunteer. They walk the talk.

Make friends wherever you go

If you're interested in medicine, go to the local health department and ask if you can volunteer. If you want to learn how to sell cars, go to a dealer and say you want to learn about the business. Offer to work for free for a couple of weeks. Be nice, and people are far more likely to help you.

Your purpose is to shadow and learn. And on the subject of selling, we all have to sell something or work for someone who does. That's a fact of life. Learning to sell is a basic life skill. Learn everything you can about selling. When you offer to volunteer, you are selling. You're selling yourself to the organization. The organization will be thinking how you can help them.

When approaching an employer or a place to volunteer it pays to know something about that organization. Do some research online first. Find out what they do and what they are trying to achieve. Think about how you can help do that. Businesses rely on their reputations. The person who interviews you will be thinking, will you be an asset or a liability, and could you be a future employee?

Dress for success

I know people who say, I don't want to cater to society. But do you want to make it, or do you want to starve? There are rules and customs for different groups. Maybe it's

"Wassup?" when you meet your friends. But it's "How are you?" at work.

You want to have a presentable look. I have one-and-a-half carat diamond earrings. I wear them sometimes, but I'm not going to wear them professionally. Socially, my diamond earrings are cool. I've seen Michael Jordan, Denzel Washington, and a host of celebrities wear them. But that's not the impression I want to give at work. Success is freedom to be yourself. Success is having choices. I have a Mohawk, and people like it. Some of my clients ask to touch it. I go on TV and speak about pet issues with my Mohawk. When you make it, you're cool. But if I was looking for a job, I wouldn't have the freedom to just be me, yet. Dress code is a uniform.

Dress appropriately. Remember, you never get a second chance to make a first impression. Most banks or businesses don't care whether you are wearing Air Jordan 1 or 15. They wouldn't be able to tell you what you're wearing on your feet. If you want to wear Air Jordans and diamond earrings, then create your own job. And that's fine. If you're selling Air Jordans, that's exactly what you want on your feet. But work culture has its own customs. Know what they are. Dress appropriately for the work environment. Dress for success.

"You can observe a lot by just watching," said baseball star Yogi Berra. In the back of my mind I'm always interviewing everywhere I go. I watch what's going on. I've been in McDonald's and asked employees if they're interested in coming to work for me. You never know who you will meet. If someone is presentable, has a good personality, work ethic, and is willing to learn, I can teach what I need. And that's true for many other employers. Attitude matters. Often, work environments change fast, so learn to be flexible and open to new ideas.

Politeness is a consideration for other people. That can win you friends and influence people. Basic manners cost nothing. Watch how people interact with each other. Observe your surroundings. How do people talk to each other? What words do they use? Notice how people communicate over the phone.

Think about your expectations from volunteering. You're not going to become an expert after a two-week volunteer experience. But maybe you can make valuable connections that will help you later on. Keep track of what you learn.

Make your own luck

People tell me I'm a lucky guy. I say yes. I'm lucky I went to school, lucky I went to college, lucky I got into one of the hardest professions to get into. I was lucky enough to work 15-hour days. I passed difficult board exams. I was lucky enough to build a 10,000 square-foot animal hospital, then lucky enough to build a second one. I was lucky enough to get 20,000 clients. I was lucky that my veterinary clinic could support me. I was lucky enough to read hundreds of books to help me learn. I was lucky enough to put that knowledge into practice. I was lucky enough to have multiple apartment buildings. I was lucky enough to make a million, lose a million, and make it back again. Yes, I've been a very lucky guy.

No doubt that luck plays a part in life. Yet, to a certain extent, you can make your own luck. And that comes from taking responsibility for what you do. There are many things in life you can't control, but there are others you can.

If you don't look for a mentor, it's unlikely you'll find one. If you don't ask, it's unlikely you'll receive. If you don't help others, why should they help you? And helping other people is the key to a successful life. Put yourself in a position to do that. There's an old saying about putting your oxygen mask on first. They tell you this when you fly in an airplane. If you're gasping for breath, how can you help the person sitting next to you? A large part of luck is being prepared to take advantage of it.

Recently, Zach Giddens from Morris Bank contacted me. Morris Bank had just opened a branch in Warner Robins. Zach walked into my office and told me he recognized me as one of the movers and shakers of this town. He wanted to earn my business and help me grow.

But I already had banking relationships. Clay is my favorite banker and he's always ready and willing to do whatever I needed. But I know it makes sense to have more than one banking relationship. Remember what happened to me in 2008? I thought about how Zach could help. I thought to myself: *Be ready to strike when the iron is hot.*

A few weeks later I called Zach. "I need a million-dollar credit card."

"What do you mean?"

"I need a million-dollar line of credit."

He said, "I think I can make it happen."

This is how I know God has a plan for me. Cathy Seymour, one of my commercial realtors, called me. She sent me down to Perry, Georgia to look at a 10 unit apartment complex. It'd only been on the market for three days. I got very excited. It was a good piece of property in a great location. But by the time I got there, somebody had already got a contract on the property. I was disappointed.

Then I overheard the realtor and the owner's granddaughter talking.

She said, "What about the big one?"

The real estate agent replied, "We haven't priced that one yet."

I asked about the property and wanted to see it.

"We don't have a price yet," said the realtor.

I just wanted to see it. So we looked at it. It's a complex of 35 townhomes. It's in a fantastic location directly across from the hospital in a great community. It'd been neglected and it was in a state of disrepair. But that's just what I was looking for. It looked like it needed at least $200,000 put into it.

I pulled the realtor aside.

"If it comes on the market, please give me the first opportunity to buy it."

I researched the project. It was taxed-assessed at somewhere around $1 million, but it was run down. I knew it could be worth between $1.5 - $2 million using the BRRRR real estate method: Buy, Rehab, Rent, Refinance, and Repeat.

Negotiation is an essential life skill. The first person to throw out a number loses. That's my rule number one. Rule number two: if the other person thinks they're winning, smile, and let them think that they won. Don't let the other person know that they lost and you won. That's a mistake.

I'm okay with the other person thinking they won. Sometimes everyone walks away thinking they won. When the realtor called me two days later, I negotiated a price way below the tax assessment. So where did I get the money?

Zach had started the ball rolling on getting my million-dollar credit card. But I needed to stall the realtor for enough time for the line of credit to be set up. I needed an extra week or so.

There is no reward without risk. I put a contract on the property but I stalled them by telling them I would be on a cruise. It was the truth, only the cruise wasn't quite as long as they thought it was. It sometimes pays to be imaginative. Zach made it happen and we got the line of credit in place just 24 hours before I closed the deal. I made it just in time, but it worked out well for both buyer and seller. Sometimes you can make your own luck.

A reason to believe

I gave Zach a reason to bet on me. On a hot July day, I drove Zach around the houses I'd rehabbed. I was selling my vision. I explained about the BRRRR method. Because I helped Zach see my vision, he believed in my dream. And that's why I earn a very good living while I sleep.

Good real estate deals won't be served up for you online, or in the newspaper. You must find them yourself, or have a relationship with a bird dog. And that's true for any business, or even finding a job. Get out and meet people. Give people a reason to believe. Look for opportunities. I would never have had this deal if I hadn't gone out looking at what was going on, and asked questions.

I will be putting a lot of money into this new acquisition. Everything in those townhouses will be new. It will be worth about $1.8 million. I could sell it now for $1.3 million. Most of my properties are paid off and are owned free and clear. I took almost 15 years to get to this point. Don't be discouraged. Start small, work hard, and follow the BRRRR method. It can happen for you. My tenants are paying off the principle on the line of credit. I'm only paying interest. My line of credit is secured by my other properties so I can refinance the loan and pay off my million-dollar credit card; then I can do it again.

Endgame

When you've been made to feel inferior your whole life, getting over it is a real struggle. Most of my life I've asked myself, am I good enough? Finally, I'm past that. For the last 20 years, I've busted my ass, sometimes working two jobs, building my veterinary business and creating a real estate empire. I've ridden storms up, I've ridden them down.

I've suffered defeat and known victory. I hit more home runs than being put out. I put many people to work and provided housing for others. I helped people, contributed to my community, and made a lot of friends.

Two years ago, I talked with Terrence about what we want to do in the next phase of our lives. He's into building and selling cars. We both want to cut back our hours. I'll never leave without making sure Critter Fixer is good and my clients are taken care of. Critter Fixer is my baby. I plan to hire more veterinarians and cut back on work a little and enjoy the fruits of my labor. I want to spend time with my son, teaching him how to become a man.

I'll always be engaged in vet med, but right now I'm busting my butt at the hospital just like I did in my twenties. I do the work of three veterinarians. I want to cut back knowing that everything is working smoothly without me.

At my stage in life, my values are evolving. I can buy things, but I want time. In 20 years, I've never been away from Critter Fixer for more than four days in a row. I don't know what it feels like to take a week away from work. I've never done it. So, what about the future? I don't have to work as hard. It's not just about the money. It's about my life plan. I'm looking for more balance.

The other day, I was looking for paint for my apartments. It's a task I enjoy. But my phone wouldn't stop ringing. Being always in demand is exhausting. I was called in two times to treat dogs for snakebites. The first ten times snakebites were exciting. I want to make sure the dog is okay, and the pet owner is too, then I want to go back and buy my paint.

Time is a nonrenewable resource. It has become more valuable. I'm willing to take a salary cut and to work less to have less stress and enjoy more. My real estate will supplement income. I want to backpack through Europe. I want to visit every football, baseball, and basketball stadium in America.

I'm realizing that less is more. What success looks like is dependent on where you are in your life plan. I want to continue my standard of living, enjoy traveling, and learn the lessons life still has in store for me. I want to teach people about business, talk to groups, and give back. I'm grateful for all the people who helped me become what I am today.

MY MESSAGE: BET ON YOURSELF.

ABOUT THE AUTHOR

Dr. Vernard L. Hodges is a veterinarian, a real estate entrepreneur, community leader, and philanthropist. He makes his home in Bonaire, GA.

Made in the USA
Columbia, SC
15 September 2019